PROLOGUE

"We all make choices, but in the end our choices make us"

- Andrew Ryan

Contents

To my family, who held through my drawdowns too.

ARCHITECTURE OF WEALTH: Build a portfolio that outlives you.

Written and edited by Ondrej Slunecko
Published by Ondřej Slunečko - 1000XPUBLISHING

Hardback ISBN: 978-80-909870-6-7
Paperback ISBN: 978-80-909870-7-4
Ebook ISBN: 978-80-909870-8-1
Keywords: investing, stock market, capital allocation, business quality, margin of safety

ARCHITECTURE OF WEALTH

Build a portfolio that outlives you.

THE COMPLETE SYSTEM BEHIND A DOCUMENTED
24% ANNUAL COMPOUND RECORD.

The Architect's Confession

In January 2018, my entire portfolio was worth about $165.

One share of Apple and a few dollars in cash. That was the whole empire.

Eight and a half years later, that account holds over $2.7 million across seven companies, next to a war chest of roughly $400,000 in cash. Total capital I ever deposited: roughly $500,000. No inheritance or lottery. Just a salary I earned, converted into permanent capital.

I am telling you this on the first page for one reason. Every claim in this book is backed by that record. You will see the positions. You will see the weights. You will see the year I lost half my money, and the year I nearly tripled it. You will see the stocks I bought like an amateur and the stocks I held like a professional. I was both, started as an amateur and I am still putting in the hours to become the investor I intent to be.

This book explains the complete system I used to build the portfolio documented in Appendix B: theory put to work, and

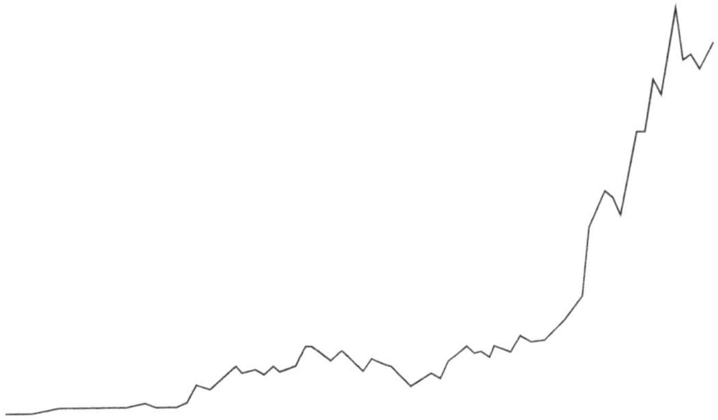

Day 1
$165

Day 3,100
$2,725,194

turned into real wealth. I am still using it today.

Two Professions, One Discipline

I moved to Denmark at eighteen to study architecture. I spent 6 years learning how buildings are made. I learned site analysis, structural calculations, material behavior and the thousand unglamorous decisions that determine whether a building will stand. The unglamorous truth that a building is decided long before anyone sees it – in the foundation, in the frame, in a thousand choices nobody photographs.

Then, in 2017, I bought my first stock. And slowly, over years, I realized something that became the spine of my life and of this book.

Architecture and investing grow from the same roots.

Both begin with a survey of the ground. Both punish shortcuts taken at the foundation. Both reward the discipline to build load-bearing structure before decoration. And both produce something with the same rare quality: permanence.

A building outlives its architect. A portfolio, built correctly, outlives its investor.

Most people treat the stock market as a slot machine with a news ticker. I treat it as an exercise in beauty. This single shift in perspective is worth more than any stock tip you will ever receive.

An architect does not panic when it rains on the site. He does not tear down the frame because a neighbor said concrete is out of fashion. He follows the drawings. He knows that the value of the structure is determined by its design and its materials, not by the weather on any given Tuesday.

You will learn to think the same way about your capital.

What I Believe

This book teaches an approach I call Contemporary Long-Term Investing. It stands on the shoulders of giants: Warren Buffett, Charlie Munger, Peter Lynch, Stanley Druckenmiller, Nick Sleep – applied to the world as it exists today.

I want to be explicit about this, because it matters: nothing in this book was conjured from nothing. Ideas are taken deliberately from certain people, the way every architect builds on foundations laid by the generation before. That is the legacy side of this craft. I built on what they left standing, and I hope, sincerely, that someone reading this page one day surpasses me.

The tools have changed. The principles have not.

The core of Contemporary Long-Term Investing fits in a few lines:

> *You buy fractional ownership of the best businesses in the world. A small number of them, seven to twelve, not fifty. You understand them deeply enough that volatility becomes weather, not danger. You keep cash ready for the moments the market loses its mind. And then you hold, for years and decades, while compounding does the heavy lifting that no amount of activity can replicate.*

Do not mistake this for passivity. This approach is intensely selective – when to buy, when to add, when to add aggressively, when a position must be trimmed, and when changed facts force an exit. Those decisions never stop. The ideal we strive toward is precise: to become investors who buy so well that we rarely need to do much afterward. The stillness is earned, not assumed.

The principle is simple, but executing it through a full market cycle is difficult. If it were easy, everyone reading this would already be wealthy, because the math has been public for a century.

> *The market transfers wealth from the incompetent to the competent, from the impatient to the patient, and from the emotional to the rational.*

Every page of this book exists to move you to the right side of those three transfers.

The Receipts

Since we will spend over two hundred pages together, you deserve to know the results of the system before you invest the hours.

From January 2018 through June 2026, my portfolio compounded at 24.2% per year, time-weighted. That is the measure of investment skill – what one dollar invested at the start became, independent of when I added money.

And the stretch matters: these were strong years for the index too, roughly 14% annually with dividends – one of the better decades passive investors will ever get. The gap of ten points a year sounds modest. Compounded, it is not: over those eight and a half years, one dollar in the index became roughly $2.90. One dollar in my portfolio became $6.20. More than double the ending wealth, earned entirely in the gap.

But the second number matters more. Measured on the actual timing of my deposits, my money-weighted return was 51.5% per year. The gap between those two numbers is not luck. It is doctrine. I held cash when the market was euphoric, and I emptied the war chest fully exactly twice – into the COVID crash of 2020 and into the bear market of 2022. The heaviest capital went in at the moments of maximum fear. That is what cash is for. To be deployed when it matters the most.

And you should also see the other side of the ledger. In my first year, I lost 52%. I owned GoPro. I owned a lingerie retailer. I owned ten positions I could not have explained to you at dinner.

I could have started the ledger in 2019 and impress you from the start. I have deliberately started it at the very beginning – the first year, the first mistakes, the version of me still finding himself. The track record in this book carries that year inside it, at full weight.

In 2022, my portfolio fell 55% from its peak, and I added to my largest position every single month while it fell. The two best years of my life (+131%, +203%) came immediately after.

I am showing you the full record, drawdowns included, because a book about investing should show the tough part. Because only after an epic journey, you can fully appreciate the destination.

And I am showing you all of it for one more reason: so you know it is possible. Eight years ago I was washing dishes in a restaurant kitchen in Denmark, studying architecture, investing what I could each month. Today I am a multimillionaire. If I could do it from a dish pit, you can do it from wherever you are standing now.

Who You Will Become

The money was the visible result, but not the only one.

Somewhere between the first share of Apple and the second million, I learned that the portfolio is not the achievement. The portfolio is the artifact. It is the physical evidence of who you had to become to build it. Patient enough to hold for eight years, rational enough to buy while bleeding, competent enough to know the difference between a falling price and a failing business.

That person is being constructed at the same time as the portfolio.

This book will make you money if you do the work. But its real ambition is larger. It is written to be handed down – from you to your children, the way the best buildings are. A structure that stands after the architect is gone. The years taught me something no return figure could: you must become capable of holding the portfolio you intend to build.

Your portfolio eventually reflects your habits: patience, discipline, judgment and the ability to act under pressure.

The ground survey begins on the next page.

Build something that lasts.

PART I: THE GROUND SURVEY

Part I, Chapter 1

Which Game Are You Playing?

"The average is just that. The average. A gilded participation trophy."

Which Game Are You Playing?

Every era has advice so universally repeated that questioning it sounds like heresy.

Ours is this: buy index funds, add money every month, never look, and in forty years you will be rich.

You have heard it from every podcast, every finance influencer, every well-meaning uncle. It is printed on the walls of the internet. And I want to begin this book by telling you something almost nobody in finance wants to admit.

That advice is technically correct. It is also the bare minimum, and you did not pick up this book to settle for that.

The Honest Case for the Index

Let me first make the argument better than its own preachers do, because I refuse to fight a strawman.

An index fund buys you the entire market for nearly nothing. No research or decisions. No emotions to manage either. There is nothing to decide. Historically it returns somewhere between six and ten percent per year over long stretches, and it beats the majority of professional fund managers after their fees. For a person who will never open an annual report, as most people never will, it may be the most effective financial product available.

If that is you, close this book, set up the automatic transfer, and live your life. I mean that with full respect. Indexing is the correct strategy for the honest majority who want no part of this craft. This book is for the minority who cannot leave it alone.

Back to index funds and their preachers. It is a strategy to prevent losing. It guarantees you the average. Every crash included, every mediocre company included, every dying business in the index included and a small fee. It is the market saying: hand over your capital, ask no questions, and accept whatever the crowd produces.

The index fund is not a wealth-building machine. It is a wealth-preserving escalator. It moves up slowly, carrying everyone who asked nothing of themselves.

The average is just that. The average. A gilded participation trophy.

The Irony at the Top

The strange thing about index-fund evangelism is who preaches it.

Warren Buffett tells the public to buy index funds. He has said it in shareholder letters read by millions. And he built one of the largest fortunes in human history by doing the exact opposite – concentrating enormous sums into a handful of businesses he studied more deeply than anyone else on earth. At ninety, more than a third of his public portfolio sat in one stock.

This is honesty about the audience. Buffett is saying: most people will not do the work, and for them, the index is the safest home. He is right. The recommendation to index is a judgment about effort, not about possibility. The moment you become someone willing to do the work, the advice was never addressed to you.

Practically everyone repeating the index gospel has made the same calculation about you that Buffett made about the general public. This book is built on the opposite assumption. It assumes you will do the work most people will not, and collect the returns most people never will.

The Menu of Games

The stock market is not one game. There are many ways to make money in it, and even more ways to lose some. Day traders scalping minutes, quants harvesting milliseconds, income investors clipping dividends, speculators riding stories, owners compounding decades: all of them operating in the same arena, playing entirely different games, by entirely different rules, with entirely different odds.

> *The market is a living ecosystem, a digital twin of the real world. Every factory, every brand, every barrel of oil and line of code, every human ambition and fear, mirrored in real time and given a price.*

Whatever exists out there there is reflected in here. Which is exactly why there is no single way to win in it, any more than there is a single way to make a living on Earth. And it is why the single most important decision you will ever make is which game, inside that ecosystem, you are playing.

1. **Day trading.** Buying and selling within hours, hunting price wiggles. You are competing against algorithms that execute in microseconds and firms that spend billions on speed. The academic data is brutal: the overwhelming majority of day traders lose money over time. It is an adrenaline subscription with a negative expected value, not a game of wealth.

2. **Swing trading, options, the exotic zoo.** Weeks-long bets on price movement, leveraged contracts, instruments most buyers cannot correctly price. Occasionally spectacular. Statistically, a wealth transfer from amateurs to professional counterparties. Every option you buy, someone

more informed sold.

3. **Passive indexing.** Offers market returns with minimal effort, but it cannot outperform the market.

4. **Long-term business ownership.** The fourth game, the oldest one, and the only one where the small player holds structural advantages. You buy fractional ownership of exceptional businesses and hold them for years while their value compounds. Your competition (funds judged quarterly, algorithms holding for milliseconds) is structurally forbidden from playing it. Time is the one edge that cannot be arbitraged away, and it is handed to you for free.

This book teaches the fourth game and only the fourth game.

And the test between them is two sentences long.

An investment is something you would still be happy to own if the market closed for five years, because the business itself pays you in growth. A speculation is anything you only own because you believe someone will pay more for it soon. Apply that test honestly and eighty percent of what retail traders do reclassifies itself instantly.

The Case for Productive Assets

Why does the ownership game work? Because a business is a productive asset, and productive assets are the only category of things that grow value from the inside. Whoever bought Netflix, Apple, or Tesla ten years ago is wealthy today for one reason, and it is not luck of the price. The businesses themselves became enormous. They serve more customers, ship more products, employ more people, and solve more problems than they did a decade ago, and their value rose because the value they produce rose.

Compare that with a bar of gold or a garage of collectibles: those can only become worth more if someone else agrees to pay more for the same fixed thing. Nothing inside them grows.

A productive business increases its value by attracting more customers, improving its products and reinvesting its profits. That is the entire case, and it is why this book concerns itself exclusively with productive assets: when you own the machine that produces the value, time itself works for you.

What the Gap Is Worth

Now the numbers, because inspiration without arithmetic is just a dream.

Take a person who starts with $10,000 and invests $1,500 every month for fifteen years.

At index returns (call it eight percent) they finish with roughly $560,000. Solid. The escalator works.

At fifteen percent (the level of a serious, improving investor) the same deposits become roughly $1,000,000.

At twenty percent (the level this book is built to train, the level of genuine competence) they finish above $1,500,000.

And in the fifteen years after that, the gap stops being a gap and becomes a different life entirely, because compounding is not linear. Every year of competence you add multiplies every year that follows.

The salary, monthly deposits and investment period are identical. Only the return changes. The difference between the outcomes is knowledge, applied with patience.

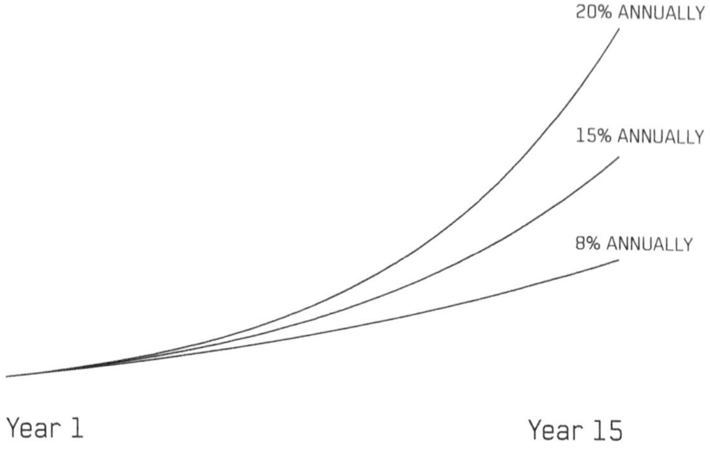

Competence, over an investing lifetime, is worth seven figures at minimum. It is the compound interest formula with different exponents.

I have lived both ends of this table, and the record is printed in the appendix of this book. My first year in the market, I lost half my money making every mistake this chapter warns against. Over the eight and a half years since, my portfolio compounded at 24.2% annually, against 14.4% for the S&P 500 index, dividends reinvested. Ten points a year does not sound like drama. Compounded on my capital, it is now measured in millions. The gap is real. I am showing you the receipts.

The Note on Inflation

One more number belongs on the table before any invitation is issued, because it forces honesty on every plan in this chapter.

Over twenty years, inflation halves the purchasing power of

money, sometimes worse. The person who believes one or two million will fund a comfortable retirement two decades from now is planning with today's prices for tomorrow's life; realistically, most people need to double or quadruple their target number.

This is one of the most underestimated facts in personal finance, and it cuts one way: average returns do not merely cap your upside. Against inflation, they barely stay ahead of the treadmill.

The Invitation

So here is the fight I am picking.

> *The index-fund gospel has convinced an entire generation that trying is irresponsible. That studying businesses is gambling, and that gambling on the average is prudence. That the ceiling is the floor and you should be grateful for it. It has taken the most powerful wealth engine ever built, ownership of great businesses, and reduced your participation to a monthly direct debit and a shrug.*

I reject that.

Indexing works, but you are capable of more, and somewhere under the layers of disclaimers, you suspect it too. That suspicion is why you picked up this book.

But be careful about which direction you take, because there are two extremes waiting for you, and both of them lose.

The side we already know: the index-and-forget crowd, who have decided that trying is not worth it and that mediocrity, delivered automatically, is an acceptable life outcome. On the other side stand the gamblers: meme stocks, meme coins, weekly options – the people who are not investing but hoping, loudly, with money they will miss. The first extreme guarantees you the average. The second usually guarantees you less than nothing.

Both extremes share the same root: neither one does the work. One refuses it out of resignation, the other skips it out of impatience.

This book threads the needle with active, calculated risk-taking: concentrated enough to outperform, but researched and sized so that a single mistake is survivable. It is more ambitious than passive indexing and more disciplined than speculation.

The market does not pay you for your effort, intelligence, or intentions. It pays you for being right about businesses and patient about time. Both of those are learnable. This book is the curriculum.

The escalator is behind you. The gambling quarter is across the street; let it keep its lights. The construction site is ahead.

Most people accept the average because nobody ever told them it was optional. Consider yourself told.

Part I, Chapter 2

The Game Is Rigged In Your Favor

"In the short run, the market is a voting machine, but in the long run, it is a weighing machine."

- Benjamin Graham

The Game Is Rigged In Your Favor

Chapter 1 picked a fight. This chapter explains why the fight is worth winning.

Because here is what the cynics and the traders miss about the stock market. Beneath the daily circus, it is the single greatest wealth-multiplication mechanism ever constructed by human beings. And it is tilted, structurally and permanently, in favor of one specific kind of participant.

The owner.

What You Buy

Strip away the tickers, the charts, the flashing red and green, and look at what a share of stock is.

> *It is a fraction of a real enterprise. Buildings, machines, patents, software, and, most valuable of all, organized groups of capable people who wake up every morning and work to make that enterprise more valuable. When you buy a share, thousands of engineers, designers, and operators are now, in a very literal sense, working partly for you. You did not hire them. You did not manage them. You simply allocated capital to them and got out of their way.*

This is the part the casino crowd never understands. A stock is not a lottery ticket that happens to have a company attached. It is a company that happens to have a price attached.

The price is quoted daily. The value is built daily.

Those are two different processes, and only one of them should command your attention.

The merit of investing, the actual social function that makes the whole machine work, is allocation of capital into the hands of people who know what to do with it.

Give the builders resources. Get out of their way.

Over years they make the world slightly better, and you are paid for having backed them. That is the oldest and most productive deal in economics.

And never lose sight of what those builders produce, because it is the entire point of the machine.

- Without Apple, there is no phone in your pocket.
- Without Novo Nordisk, a hundred million diabetics are rationing insulin.
- Without Netflix, you are driving to a rental store for a plastic disc.
- Without TSMC, there are no chips in your phone, your car, your hospital, or your missile defense.
- Without Amazon, you are spending Saturday driving between three stores.
- Without Spotify, your music collection fits in a shoebox and skips when the car hits a bump.
- Without Tesla, the electric car is still a golf cart with ambitions.
- Without SpaceX, rockets do not land themselves on barges, and orbit still costs a nation's ransom.
- Without Uber, you are standing in the rain, hoping.
- Without Google, the answer to your question is in a library, closed on Sundays.

If companies do not produce things, there are no things.

Companies are how human life improves. They turn inventions into things ordinary people can use and afford. When you buy a share, you are tying your future to the CEO and to every engineer and worker inside that enterprise. Choose ones worth being tied to.

Why the Board Tilts Upward

Now the structural part.

Why does the market, as a whole, rise over long periods?

Not as an article of faith, but as a consequence of four forces, each one independent, all four pushing the same direction.

1. **Value creation.** Companies that grow their revenue, profits, and free cash flow become more valuable. This is the engine. Human beings keep inventing and compounding knowledge, and enterprises are the vehicle through which that progress becomes ownable. As long as people keep improving things, and they have never stopped, the aggregate value of enterprise rises.

2. **Inflation.** Governments print money, slowly in normal decades and rapidly in strange ones. Every printed dollar dilutes cash and inflates the nominal price of real assets. Productive businesses are real assets. The saver holding cash is taxed by this every year; the owner of enterprises is subsidized. You do not have to like this arrangement. You only have to notice which side of it you are standing on.

3. **Growth.** Populations expand, productivity compounds, new markets open. GDP grinds upward across decades, recessions notwithstanding, and corporate earnings ride that grind. Betting on the

long-term market is, at root, betting that humanity will keep producing more than it did last year. That bet has paid for two centuries.

4. **The state itself.** Here is the cynical force, and it is the most reliable of the four. Governments collect taxes on capital gains. Pension systems are wired into equity markets. The retirement of entire nations depends on stocks rising over time. The most powerful institutions on earth are, structurally, long. They do not always succeed in the short run, no one does, but you want to notice when your position and the state's incentives point the same direction.

Four forces. All compounding. All indifferent to this quarter's headlines.

The game is rigged, ever so slightly, in favor of the patient owner. Your only job is to refuse to be shaken off the board.

The Two Sides of Every Trade

Rigged in your favor does not mean charitable. The same machine that multiplies wealth also redistributes it, ruthlessly, every single day. For every trade there are two parties, one of them is making a mistake.

The market transfers wealth from the impatient to the patient. The impatient sell in October because the summer was scary; the patient buy what they sell, and collect the recovery. It transfers wealth from the emotional to the rational: panic is, mechanically, an asset sale at the worst available price, and someone rational is standing on the other side of it.

And it transfers wealth from the ignorant to the informed, the person who owns a ticker because of a tweet will eventually sell it to a person who read the filings, at precisely the wrong moment, for precisely the wrong reason.

This is not a modern cruelty of markets. It is one of the oldest patterns there is, called the Matthew Effect, after a line written two thousand years ago: "For whoever has will be given more, and they will have an abundance. Whoever does not have, even what they have will be taken from them."

The market did not invent the transfer. It only runs it faster.

Millionaires

Twenty-four million millionaires live in the United States.

Overwhelmingly, they got there through one of three vehicles: a business, real estate, or the stock market.

The first requires an idea, obsession, and years of your life. The second requires leverage and landlording. The third requires a brokerage account, capital, and knowledge.

It is the only wealth vehicle in history that is fully open to anyone with a phone, the same Palantir shares, at the same price, whether you are a pension fund or a student in a dorm.

The market does not check your credentials. It checks your behavior. That is what open access means: the door is unlocked, and so is the trapdoor.

Weather and Climate

One more mental model completes the foundation, and I will lean on it for the rest of the book.

The daily market is weather. Elections, rate decisions, earnings reactions, corrections, the red day that ruins a Tuesday. Weather. Loud and dramatic, at the distance of a decade, almost meaningless. The long-term trajectory of great businesses is climate: quiet, statistical, overwhelming and inevitable.

Every catastrophe of the last century, wars, oil shocks, a pandemic that closed the planet, is now a barely visible dent in the long-term chart of the market. Every single one felt like the end of the world in real time. The investors who were ruined were almost never ruined by the events. They were ruined by their reaction to the events: selling the climate because of the weather.

It might happen that you buy a great company the week before a crash. Nobody can prevent this, and nobody can predict it – not you, not me, not anyone paid to pretend otherwise. But a great company sails through the storm and returns stronger, because that is what you selected it for. The storm was never the risk.

What the risk is, and why almost everyone defines it exactly backwards, is the subject of the next two chapters.

The game is rigged in your favor. The house wants you to win. All it asks is the one thing most players cannot give it.

Stay at the table.

Part I, Chapter 3

The Investing Trifecta

"My wealth has come from a combination of living in America, some lucky genes, and compound interest."

- Warren Buffett

The Investing Trifecta

Every fortune ever built in the stock market, every single one, from Buffett's to the anonymous millionaire next door, was built from exactly three ingredients.

Capital. Growth rate. Time.

That is the complete list. There is no fourth ingredient, no secret variable, no exotic instrument that adds a term to the equation.

Compounding is a machine with three dials, and your entire career as an investor is the management of those three dials. So before we touch a single stock, we are going to understand the machine, including the part almost nobody tells beginners, which is that the dial you should focus on changes as you grow.

CAPITAL DEPLOYED × CAGR × TIME = WEALTH

The Three Dials

Capital is the fuel, what you feed the machine, from income and discipline. In the beginning it is everything. A fifty percent return on a $2,000 portfolio is $1,000; a disappointing year of saving beats a spectacular year of investing at this size.

> *This is why the early stage must be brute-forced: earn more, spend less, feed the machine relentlessly.*

For calibration: in my first year I invested roughly $14,000. And I was just a student, washing dishes in a restaurant, in 2018. Call it a thousand dollars a month, extracted from a dish pit. I mention this as a bar: if a student on kitchen wages could feed the machine a thousand a month in 2018, you can, at minimum, match that today. The fuel was never the hard part. Deciding you are the kind of person who supplies it is.

Growth rate is the engine, what your capital earns per year, on average, across decades. This is the competence dial, the only one of the three that responds to knowledge. It is also the dial with the most violent long-term consequences, as you are about to see.

Time is the multiplier. The number of years the engine runs uninterrupted. It is the most powerful dial and the least respected, because its effects are invisible for years and then suddenly overwhelming. Time cannot be bought, borrowed, or accelerated. It can only be protected, which is why every behavior that interrupts compounding, from panic selling to constant portfolio renovation, is an attack on your most valuable asset.

What the Growth Dial Is Worth

Now the table that justifies this entire book. Take a person starting with $10,000, adding $1,500 every month, for fifteen years – an ordinary professional with ordinary discipline.

Annual return, after 15 years

10%	roughly the index	$640,000
15%	a solid, improving investor	$950,000
20%	a competent investor	$1,450,000

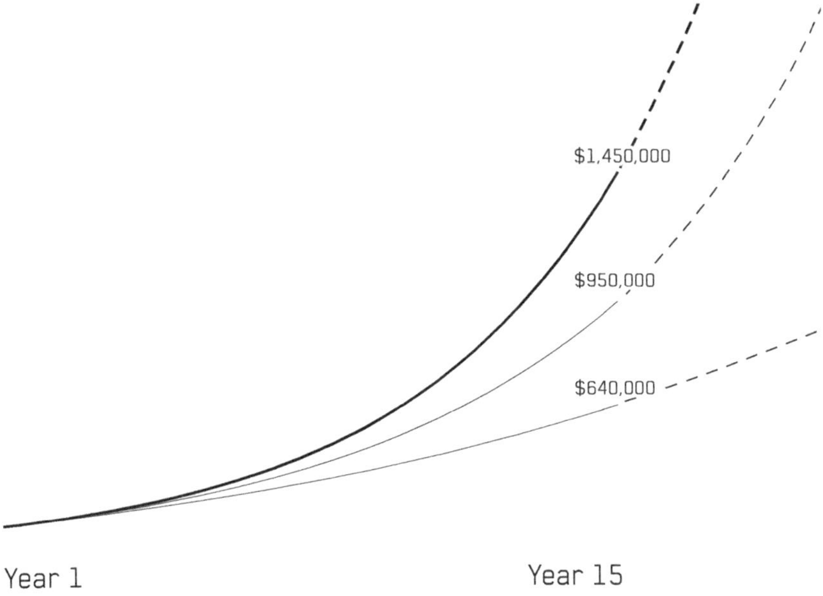

- Same person.
- Same deposits.
- Same fifteen years.

The only difference between the rows is knowledge, and the difference between the first row and the last is roughly $800,000. That is what competence pays for an ordinary investor over a single fifteen-year stretch.

But the table understates the truth, because compounding is not linear. Run the same three scenarios another ten years and the gap explodes from hundreds of thousands into many millions. Every point of annual return you add multiplies every year that remains in front of you. This is why learning this craft in your twenties or thirties is one of the highest-paying activities available to a human being: you are not earning a return on money. You are earning a return on every future year at once.

Rank it against the prestige professions and the point

sharpens. A competent investor's skill compounds like a doctor's salary never will, scales like a lawyer's hours never can, and, unlike almost every other high-value profession, it works without clients, without employees, and without permission. A great salesperson earns on every deal; a great investor earns on every dollar, forever.

Investing competence ranks on par with any of those careers, and past a certain portfolio size, above them. It is the rare skill that pays better than the job that funded it.

For calibration: over the eight and a half years covered in this book's appendix, my own portfolio compounded at 24.2% which demonstrates the dial's range is real.

The Sequence of Focus

Here is the strategic insight the trifecta produces, and it will organize the entire structure of this book.

Below roughly $100,000, capital is the main dial. Your savings rate moves the portfolio more than your skill does. So the correct behavior is aggressive feeding.

- Maximize income
- Minimize expenses
- Deposit relentlessly

All that while building knowledge in parallel for the stage ahead. Do the learning now, precisely because it does not pay much yet. By the time it pays, it must already be built.

From six figures to seven, growth rate takes over. Contributions still matter, but skill now moves more money than savings do. A 20% year on $400,000 is $80,000, more than most people can save. This is where the competence you built in stage one starts collecting its salary, and where the chapters of Part II and Part III become the highest-leverage hours of your financial life.

Beyond seven figures, time and temperament rule. Deposits become rounding errors. Skill matures. What remains is the discipline to let the machine run – the refusal to interrupt, which sounds trivial and is in fact the rarest skill in markets. Part IV of this book lives entirely on this dial.

Most investors fail by working the wrong dial for their stage: the beginner obsessing over stock picks while depositing $100 a month, or the millionaire still churning positions for action when his only remaining job is to sit still.

The Machine Does Not Negotiate

One warning before we move on. The trifecta is symmetric, and it compounds mistakes with the same indifference it compounds gains.

A lost year is not one year of returns, it is that year multiplied by every year that would have followed it. A catastrophic loss at forty costs incomparably more than the same loss at twenty-five, because it destroys capital and time together. This is why Part I of this book spends so long on risk before ever discussing what to buy: the first commandment of compounding is not "grow fast." It is "never interrupt."

> *Capital you control through discipline. Growth rate you control through competence. Time you control through behavior.*

Three dials. All three are yours. That fact, that nothing here belongs to Wall Street or to luck, is either terrifying or liberating.

Choose liberating. Then start feeding the machine.

Part I, Chapter 4

Risk Is Ignorance, Not Volatility

"In fact, you can argue that if you're not willing to react with equanimity to a market price decline of 50% two or three times a century, you're not fit to be a common shareholder and you deserve the mediocre result you're going to get."

- Charlie Munger.

Risk Is Ignorance, Not Volatility

In 2022, my portfolio fell fifty-five percent.

Not on paper in some abstract sense, in the account, in numbers I looked at every day, for twelve consecutive months. A grinding, relentless bear market took my capital from a quarter of a million at the peak to barely half of that by December. Friends asked, carefully, if I was okay. Whether I was going to do something.

I did do something. I bought. Every single month, all year. And I slept, and I slept well, because of a single definition I had installed years earlier, the most valuable definition in all of investing:

Volatility is not risk. Risk is permanent loss of capital.

> *The entire financial industry defines risk as volatility, as the wiggle of the price, measured, modeled, and sold back to you as beta and standard deviation. This definition is convenient for people who write academic papers and manage other people's money by the quarter. For the individual investor building wealth over decades, it is not only wrong. It is inverted. It teaches you to fear the thing that pays you and ignore the thing that kills you.*

This chapter re-installs the correct definition. Everything else in the book depends on it.

Weather Versus Structural Failure

Return to the building.

A skyscraper sways. It is designed to sway, engineers give tall buildings meters of movement at the top, because a rigid structure snaps in wind that a flexible one shrugs off. No architect on earth looks at a swaying tower in a storm and calls it risk. The sway is the design working.

Structural failure is another category entirely. A cracked foundation. Corroded rebar. Load miscalculated by someone who did not do the analysis. Buildings do not fall because of wind. They fall because of what was wrong before the wind arrived.

Your portfolio swinging twenty percent in a year is sway. If you own strong businesses, it is not risk in any meaningful sense. It is the designed response of a market structure to the weather of human emotion. The stock of a wonderful company can fall by half while the company itself grows revenue every quarter. Price and value disconnect all the time; the disconnection is temporary, noisy, and, for the prepared, profitable.

Permanent loss is structural. It happens when the business itself fails: when revenue collapses, when the moat is breached, when management destroys the capital you handed them. Or, more commonly, when the investor converts temporary sway into permanent loss with one action: selling at the bottom, because the sway felt like falling.

Nobody can tell the difference between sway and structural failure by watching the price. The price looks identical in both cases: red. The difference lives in one place only, your knowledge of the business.

And that is why risk is ignorance. Not volatility. Ignorance.

What Risk Looks Like

Buffett said it in one line: risk comes from not knowing what you are doing. Let me make the line concrete, because real risk has specific faces, and not one of them is a price chart.

- Risk is dilution: management printing new shares year after year, cutting your slice of the pie while the headline stock price distracts you.
- Risk is misaligned incentives: executives paid for short-term stock pops, harvesting the company you own for their own exit.
- Risk is poor execution: strategies that never ship, acquisitions that never integrate, promises rolled forward every quarter.
- Risk is a deteriorating moat: the competitive advantage you bought eroding while the brand name keeps the price afloat for two more years.
- Risk is buying at a price so far above value that even a good business needs a decade to grow into it.
- Risk is a thesis drift: the company you own today no longer being the company you researched, while you never noticed because you never re-checked.

Notice the shared property of every item on that list. All of them are knowable. Every one is visible in filings, in earnings calls, in the numbers, before it becomes fatal, to an investor who does the work. None of them appear in a volatility measure. A stock can have a placid, low-beta chart while dilution eats it alive, and a violent, terrifying chart while the underlying business compounds beautifully.

The market does not forgive ignorance. It prices it, and it collects, from someone, on every trade. Eliminating risk is impossible. Research cannot eliminate uncertainty. It can eliminate ignorance. You are paid for accepting the first and punished for tolerating the second.

The industry's definition tells you a diversified basket of businesses you know nothing about is safe. My definition tells you that is the riskiest structure you can build: a portfolio where, on the day the storm comes, you have no way to tell sway from collapse, so you will sell everything, at the bottom, to make the fear stop.

2022, From the Inside

The 2022 bear market put that definition to the test.

The year was a slow-motion avalanche. Inflation, rate hikes, fear stacked on fear, twelve months of nearly uninterrupted decline. My largest position, Palantir, fell from eighteen dollars to $6.42. The portfolio was cut in half. On the screen, it was indistinguishable from catastrophe.

So I did what the screen cannot do. I checked the structure.

Revenue: growing, every quarter. Customers: multiplying. The balance sheet: fortress, billions in cash, no debt. Margins: expanding along exactly the trajectory I had underwritten two years earlier. The engineering report and the price were telling opposite stories, and I had done enough work to know which one was lying. The price was reacting to interest rates and mood. The business had never been stronger.

The same inspection ran across the whole portfolio, position by position, every month. Tesla: sway. Meta: sway, plus a self-inflicted spending problem worth monitoring. Monitoring, not fleeing. Nothing structural. So nothing was sold. The reserve deployed instead, month after month, into the fear.

And the ending? The next two years were spectacular. Plus 131%, plus 203%, the two best years of my life, delivered directly to whoever owned those assets on the morning the weather turned. Investors who sold in December 2022 converted a temporary decline into a permanent loss and surrendered the recovery to the buyers on the other side.

The market bottom was not the moment of maximum danger. It was the moment of minimum danger and maximum fear. Those two peaks almost never occur together, and the entire fortune of the long-term investor is made in the gap between them.

The Toll

I will not pretend the definition makes the experience painless, and you should distrust anyone who does.

Watching half your net worth evaporate over twelve months hurts – physically, at three in the morning, in conversations with people who love you and think you have lost your mind.

Knowledge does not switch the pain off.

What knowledge does is contain it: the pain becomes something you merely observe, the way a meditator observes a thought – it arrives, it announces itself, it passes through, and it leaves without being obeyed. Meditation never promises an empty mind, only a mind that recognizes thoughts as visitors.

This is the same discipline with money attached: the pain stays an emotion instead of becoming an instruction. You feel it, you inspect the structure, the structure holds, and you do not sell. That sequence, feel-verify-hold, is the entire skill, and it cannot be faked in the moment. It is built in calm years or not at all.

I learned this in a ring before I ever learned it in a market. The fighters who panic are not the ones who take the hardest shots. They are the ones who have never been hit before. The first real body shot is information: it tells you that you can be hit, and stand, and keep your hands up.

A bear market is a body shot with your net worth behind it. You do not want the first one to arrive untested. Take a few in practice, with small money, in years that do not matter, so that when a real one lands you already know the difference between hurt and finished.

Hurt is a price falling; finished is a business failing. On the screen they look identical, red, and the only thing that tells them apart is the work you did before the bell rang.

> *Because here is the honest contract of this profession. Volatility is not a bug you endure on the way to returns. Volatility is why the returns exist. The market pays equity holders several points a year more than bondholders for exactly one service: carrying the sway that others cannot stomach. Remove the volatility and you remove the payment, that instrument exists, and it is called a savings account.*

Severe drawdowns are part of earning long-term equity returns. You cannot collect the full upside while avoiding every period of fear.

Most people pay the toll and then turn back a kilometer before the destination.

Know what you own. That is the whole risk model. Everything the industry sells you beyond it is a measurement of weather by people who have never checked a foundation.

Part I, Chapter 5

The Edge Nobody Can Take From You

"Play long-term games with long-term people."

- Naval Ravikant

The Edge Nobody Can Take From You

Every market participant is hunting for an edge, and almost every edge has been hunted to extinction.

Speed? Algorithms execute in microseconds; you will never be faster. Information? An army of analysts parses every filing within minutes of release; you will never know first. Access? The days of retail investors being systematically last in line for data are over, but so are the days of finding anything the professionals have not seen.

And yet two edges remain: enormous and structural, still available to you. The first, the professionals are forbidden from using. The second, most of them never learned.

Time, and interpretation.

Why Wall Street Cannot Hold

Understand who you are competing against, because their constraints are your opportunity.

A professional fund manager is graded every quarter. Underperform for four of them and clients withdraw; underperform for eight and the career is over. It does not matter that his five-year thesis is correct, he will not be employed in five years to collect on it. So he does the rational thing for his career: he hugs the benchmark, buys what is already popular, and sells anything that might embarrass him at the next review.

And notice that the professionals are mostly following each other: the same conferences, the same models, the same consensus. The herd behavior you were warned about in retail investing runs the institutions too, sheep in suits.

The industry even has a name for the disease, career risk.

It forces brilliant people into mediocre decisions, structurally, forever.

Algorithms are worse. The machines that dominate daily volume hold positions for minutes, hours, sometimes milliseconds. They are magnificent at extracting pennies from the next tick and constitutionally incapable of caring what a business earns in 2031.

Now notice what this means. The most well-resourced participants in the market are all crowded into the same short time horizon, fighting each other for scraps, while the returns that come from holding a great business for a decade sit almost uncontested.

Wall Street rents stocks by the quarter. You are trying to own decades. You are not playing against them. You are playing a game they are not allowed to enter.

The Bar Is on the Floor

You have probably heard the discouraging statistic: the great majority of investors, commonly cited near 95%, fail to beat the market over time. Here is the reframe that statistic deserves: it counts retail and professionals alike, and it describes the same ruthless arithmetic either way.

Returns follow a power law. The top slice of investors harvests most of the excess return, and the bottom four-fifths fight over what remains. Your goal is to be in the top slice. Retail or institutional is irrelevant; competent or not is the only census that pays.

Now the silver lining: look at what the average participant does.

They buy whatever was pitched on television. They buy a ticker a friend mentioned, or one a video recommended, and they do not read a single filing before or after. That is the competition, that is the 95%.

> *Which means the bar to be exceptional is lying on the floor, and still, somehow, most people trip over it. If you do the work at all (read the statements, re-verify the thesis) you are ahead of nine out of ten participants by default. Do the work well, consistently, for years, and the top few percent stops being a dream and becomes a math problem.*

Eight Years of One Company

Theory again, so here is the receipt.

In February 2018, a month into my investing life, I bought one share of Tesla for $349. One share. It was most of what I could afford.

What followed was everything the market can throw at a holder. Production hell and bankruptcy headlines in 2018. A drawdown that made the position look foolish for a year. Then a run so violent the stock split five-for-one in 2020 and three-for-one in 2022. Then 2022 itself, when the shares fell by two thirds while the internet held a funeral. I added on the way: 21 shares in 2019 when conviction grew, more through the splits and the crashes. Today the position stands at 680 shares, held for eight and a half years and counting, worth more than a quarter of a million dollars.

Here is the honest question: was I certain in 2018 that this would happen? No. Nobody was, and anyone who claims otherwise is selling something. What I had was a thesis about where the world was going, a company positioned at the center of it, and, the actual edge, the willingness to let eight years pass while the thesis played out.

What I needed was to be directionally correct, and I was, but never blindly. I did not close my eyes and hold. I re-underwrote the position every quarter for eight years: the earnings calls, the income statement, the balance sheet, the delivery numbers. There were rough waters, and I knew exactly how rough, because I was checking. What the checking kept confirming was that the operating business remained on a positive long-term trajectory, and that is what licensed the holding.

Conviction without verification is just stubbornness with a brokerage account.

Hundreds of thousands of people bought Tesla before I did and made nothing, because owning it was never the hard part. Every fortune that stock produced went exclusively to the people who did not leave.

Nick Sleep, one of the great investors of our era, understood this better than anyone. His fund's returns came overwhelmingly from a handful of businesses, Costco, Amazon, identified early and then simply held, for a decade and more, while other smart people traded in and out of the same names collecting fractions of the outcome. His observation was that the destination of a great business is knowable years in advance; what is scarce is not the insight but the patience to travel there.

Time in a great company is not waiting. It is the position working.

The Second Edge: Interpretation

Everyone stares at the same data. The filings are public, the numbers arrive for all of us on the same afternoon. So the edge was never access to information; that war is over, and everyone lost equally.

The edge is what you build from it, the interpretation.

Investing is part science and part art, and this is precisely where the art lives. The science collects the data points; the art infers the future from them, and inference is not extrapolation.

A line on a chart does not continue because it has been going up, and the analyst who simply extends last year's growth rate into the next decade is doing arithmetic, not thinking.

The real work is creative: given these numbers, this management, this industry, what future paths are plausible? What has to be true for each? Which does the current price assume?

> *Two investors can hold identical spreadsheets and reach opposite conclusions, and one of them will be paid for the difference. The market is an interpretation contest, and interpretation, unlike information, cannot be commoditized.*

Compounding Needs Runway

There is a mathematical reason the last years matter most, and it is worth seeing plainly.

> *A portfolio compounding at 20% doubles roughly every 3.6 years. Which means a 25-year investing life contains about seven doublings, and the final doubling adds more dollars than the previous six combined.*

Cut the runway short by five years, through impatience or interruption, and you do not lose five years of average returns. You lose the largest years, the ones at the end, the ones the entire journey existed to reach.

This is why the decade-scale horizon is not a stylistic preference. It is where the money physically is. And it is why every force in modern financial culture, quarterly earnings theater, daily price alerts, the entire attention economy of market media is a machine for talking you out of your only edge. Every headline that makes you act is transferring your runway to someone else.

Somewhere in 2040, there is a version of you looking back at this decade. From that terrace, all of it (the elections, the rate decisions, the corrections that felt like emergencies) will have faded into a single smooth line moving up and to the right. The only question that version of you will care about is embarrassingly simple: did you stay in the game?

Hold that image. We will return to it at the very end of this book.

The market is a device for transferring money from the impatient to the patient. You cannot out-trade the machines and you cannot out-research Wall Street.

You can out-wait everyone, and you can out-interpret the consensus about what the data means. Those two edges, compounded together, are the entire game. So play them.

Part I, Chapter 6

Prerequisites

"Everyone has the brainpower to make money in stocks. Not everyone has the stomach."

- Peter Lynch

Prerequisites: The Building Permit

No serious construction begins without a permit, and no serious portfolio should either.

This is the shortest chapter in Part I, and the one most readers will be tempted to skip. Do not. Every catastrophic investing story I have heard began with a violation of something on this page. Every one ends with someone leaving the market forever. The market did not destroy those people. Their conditions did.

Four conditions. Check all four before a single dollar goes in.

1. The Emergency Fund Stands Apart

Before you invest, you hold three to six months of living expenses in cash. Boring, instantly accessible, and completely separate from your portfolio and from your war chest.

The reason is structural. The single greatest destroyer of long-term returns is the forced sale: the moment life demands money (a medical bill, a lost job, a broken car) and the only source is your portfolio, at whatever price the market happens to be quoting that week. Murphy's law of markets says that week will be the bottom. The emergency fund exists so that no event in your life can ever force your hand in the market. It converts every future crisis from a portfolio event into a mere inconvenience.

An investor who can never be forced to sell has already eliminated the most common cause of permanent loss.

Full disclosure: I once violated this rule myself. In the COVID crash of 2020 I went all in: everything, including money that prudence says should have stayed in reserve. It worked, and I still do not fully endorse it, because look at what made it survivable: I was a student. No family, no dependents, nobody relying on me, and honestly nothing to lose, the downside of ruin was eating cheap pasta for another year. That is the one life stage where excess risk is at least arguable. If anyone depends on you, the rule stands exactly as written.

2. No Expensive Debt

Credit card balances and consumer loans at fifteen or twenty-five percent interest are a compounding machine running against you, a guaranteed negative return that no realistic portfolio can outrun. Investing while carrying such debt is filling a bathtub with the drain open. Kill the expensive debt first; it is the highest guaranteed return available to you anywhere. Reasonable, low-interest debt (a sensible mortgage) is a different category and can coexist with investing.

And yes, there are ways to use reasonable debt on productive assets to genuine advantage, but understand that this is a different game requiring its own skill: the discipline of leverage, its costs, its failure modes. It is largely beyond the scope of this book.

I personally prefer to carry no debt at all, and I understand those who choose otherwise; just treat that choice as a craft to be studied, never as free money.

3. Stable Income

The strategy in this book runs on regular contributions and a fillable war chest. Both require income that reliably exceeds expenses. If that is not yet true, the highest-return project in your life is not stock selection, it is your career and your cost structure. Fix the cash flow engine first. The market will still be here.

4. The Stomach

The last prerequisite is the one nobody can check for you.

Over the next fifteen years, this strategy guarantees that you will watch your portfolio fall 30 to 50% at least once or twice, over months, while every voice around you says it is different this time. You have read Chapter 4 and you understand intellectually that this is sway, not collapse. But understanding is not the same as enduring.

Some people, honest and intelligent people, are simply not built to watch numbers fall without acting, and for them, the honest answer is the one Tenet 25 gives: index, automate, and sleep well.

> *Anyone has the brainpower to make money in stocks. Not everyone has the stomach, and pretending is the most expensive form of self-deception in finance.*

There is no shame in either answer. There is only shame in discovering the answer for the first time at the bottom of a bear market, with real money.

Set the Target Before You Pour

One more thing belongs in the permit, and it is a destination, not a number.

Do not enter the market with an abstract dream.

"I want to be a millionaire someday" is a whimsy mood.

Enter with a target that has a number and a date: I am at $40,000 today, I can invest $1,500 a month, and I intend to reach $2 million within eighteen years. That sentence is a blueprint. It tells you the growth rate you need, which tells you the competence you must build, which tells you what to do this year. And when reality drifts from the plan, as it will, you adjust the plan deliberately instead of drifting with your feelings.

> *Set the target high. Outrageous targets on expanded timelines are, strangely, more realistic than modest ones on short timelines, because compounding does its greatest work in the years that timid plans cut off. Twenty years of ordinary discipline beats five years of heroic ambition in every simulation that has ever been run.*

A personal note on calibration: I set my goals ambitious, extraordinary, but not impossible. The shape I aim for is a target where hitting it is world-class, and falling twenty percent short is still a result most people would celebrate. There are many ways to set goals. That one has never failed me.

That is the entire permit. An untouchable reserve, no expensive debt, positive cash flow, an honest stomach, and a dated target.

None of it is glamorous. Neither is a foundation. You will notice, though, that nobody standing in a finished building ever complains about the months spent below ground.

Permits issued. The foundation pour begins in Part II.

PART II: THE FOUNDATION

Part II, Chapter 7

Concentration: The Mathematics of Conviction

"Diversification is what you buy when you have run out of conviction."

Concentration: The Mathematics of Conviction

"Diversification is protection against ignorance."

Warren Buffett said that at a Berkshire Hathaway shareholder meeting. At ninety years old, he held over one third of his public portfolio in a single stock: Apple. The man who tells the public to buy index funds built the greatest investment fortune in history through concentrated bets on a handful of businesses he understood better than anyone alive.

Read his sentence again, because most people hear it backwards. He is not insulting diversification. He is defining it.

Diversification is what you do when you do not know.

It is the rational strategy for the ignorant, and he means ignorant literally, not cruelly. If you will not study businesses, you should own hundreds of them and accept the average.

But the sentence contains a door, and almost nobody walks through it.

> *If diversification is protection against ignorance, then knowledge is permission to concentrate.*

This chapter is about earning that permission, and then using it. It is the load-bearing wall of this entire book, and Part III is where you will forge the load-bearing skills that hold it up.

Reading financial statements, valuing businesses, running projections: every one of them exists to justify what this chapter proposes. Owning few things, in size, for a long time.

The Math Nobody Runs

Start with the number that should end the debate.

Joel Greenblatt, a fund manager who compounded at rates most professionals consider fictional, proved it mathematically during his years in academia. By holding just eight companies, you eliminate 81% of the single-stock risk compared to owning one. By sixteen stocks, you have eliminated around 93%. After that, each additional position buys you almost nothing.

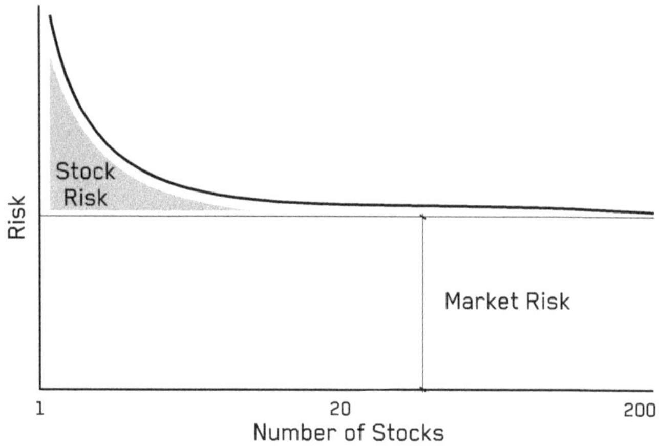

The risk-reduction benefit of diversification is almost entirely captured by the first eight to twelve holdings. Position number twenty-five does not protect you. Position number forty does not protect you. They only guarantee one thing: that your results converge toward the average, minus your effort.

This produces two failure modes, and they sit on opposite ends of the same ruler.

Below roughly seven positions, you are being irrational. The risk reduction from seven or eight uncorrelated quality businesses is nearly free. It costs you almost no expected return, and it protects you from the one scenario that ends the game; permanent, concentrated, unrecoverable loss. Refusing that protection is reckless.

Above roughly twenty positions, you have changed professions. You are no longer an investor. You are an underfunded index fund with worse tax treatment. Every position past that line forces you to deploy capital into your fifteenth-best idea, then your twentieth-best idea. Nobody has twenty great ideas. The twentieth idea is the one you jotted down during lunch to fill space.

The optimal range for a portfolio is seven to twelve companies. The best businesses in their industries. The number one player wherever possible. One company allowed to grow to as much as a third of your capital, if, and only if, it has earned it.

> *We are looking for crème de la crème, and refusing everything else.*

The Closet Index

Here is the most common portfolio mistake I encounter.

Fifty to sixty positions. Assembled over years from newsletters, podcasts, a friend's tip, a headline, a hunch. Each position is one to three percent. The owner can explain perhaps six of them. Asked why they own position number thirty-eight, the honest answer is: someone mentioned it in 2021.

This portfolio has a name. It is a closet index fund, except worse. An index fund charges you 0.03% and demands nothing. The closet index charges you your evenings, your attention, and your anxiety, and then delivers index-like returns anyway, because sixty positions mathematically cannot do anything else. All of the effort of active investing. None of the reward.

If this is your portfolio, the fix is better judgment, the willingness to rank. These five positions are my best ideas. These forty are not. And then acting on the ranking, which is the part that hurts.

> *Concentration is not primarily a buying decision. It is a refusing decision. You concentrate by saying no ninety-nine times, so that the one yes matters.*

Anatomy of a Conviction Position

Theory is cheap, so let me show you the real thing, from my own records, month by month. This is the position that built the majority of my net worth, and more importantly, this is what the process looks like from the inside, because from the outside people only ever see the ending.

In October 2020, I bought my first 160 shares of Palantir Technologies at around ten dollars. The company had just gone public. It was unprofitable. Most of Wall Street dismissed it as an overhyped government contractor. What I saw, after doing the work, was different: software with genuine switching costs, a founder-led team playing a decades-long game, and, critically, a business whose economics implied enormous margins once it scaled. The profits did not exist yet. The architecture for them did.

160 shares. A starter position. Because conviction is constructed in stages.

Through 2021, I kept adding as I kept learning: 350 shares, then 510, then 640 as the price drifted down through the twenties. By December 2021, I held 1,440 shares at around eighteen dollars, and I was underwater.

Then came 2022. The stock did not decline. It collapsed. Eighteen dollars became thirteen, became nine, became eight. By December 2022, Palantir traded at $6.42 – down roughly 85 percent from its hype-cycle peak. The internet declared it dead. The financial press wrote its obituary quarterly.

Here is my purchase record for that year:

Month (2022)	Shares Held	Price
January	2,700	$13.71
March	3,700	$13.73
May	5,200	$8.68
August	6,500	$7.72
October	8,350	$8.79
December	9,600	$6.42

I bought through the collapse. My total portfolio fell 55% that year, and I directed nearly every dollar of fresh capital into the position falling hardest. From the outside, this looked like madness. From the inside, it was the calmest year of my investing life, because the thing I was watching was not the price. Revenue kept growing. Commercial customers kept multiplying. The margin structure I had underwritten in 2020 kept materializing, quarter after quarter, while the stock told a completely different story.

The price said the building was on fire. The engineering report said the foundation had never been stronger. When those two disagree, the entire question of your investing life is: which one have you done enough work to believe?

I made my final purchases in early 2023 in the seven-to-eight dollar range, with a last addition at fifteen. Twelve thousand shares. And then I did nothing. This is the part nobody writes books about. Not one share bought or sold in the three years since.

Today those shares trade above $115. The position is worth over $1.4 million and represents roughly half of my portfolio.

The Second Decision

That last fact deserves its own section, because it is where most investors who get everything else right still fail.

Palantir did not become half of my portfolio because I bought recklessly. At the time of my final purchase, it was a large position, but a proportionate one. It became half of my portfolio by appreciating twelve-fold while I refused to interfere.

Understand this clearly: concentration is chosen twice. Once when you buy, and again, every single day, when you decline to trim a winner back to a "sensible" weight.

The conventional advice screams at you to rebalance. Take profits. Nobody ever went broke taking a profit. And it is true: nobody went broke that way. Nobody got wealthy that way either. Peter Lynch called it cutting the flowers and watering the weeds: systematically selling your proven best business to fund your mediocre ones, in the name of tidiness.

A position that grows into dominance has done something profound. It has proven its thesis with years of evidence, in public, with your own money. That position has earned more of your capital, not less. The company that earns a place in your portfolio through appreciation passed a harder exam than any new purchase ever could.

Do I feel the weight of it? Every day. A ten percent decline in that one position is a six-figure day. This is the sleep test, and it is not theoretical at this scale. But the sleep test is not a question about your portfolio. It is a question about your knowledge. I sleep well because I have read every quarterly report for six years, and I know precisely what I own and why.

If a position that size would keep you awake, the answer is deeper work, or honest acknowledgment that this game, at this intensity, is not yours to play.

Both answers are respectable. Only pretending is expensive.

The License Has Conditions

Now the warning, and I need you to take it as seriously as everything above.

> *Everything in this chapter is conditional on competence. Concentration does not create returns. Concentration amplifies judgment, in whichever direction it points.*

Concentrate with knowledge, and you get the record you just read. Concentrate with ignorance, and you get the same story with the opposite ending: the man who put half his net worth into a stock he heard about on a podcast, rode it down 90%, and learned that the market does not grade effort or sincerity. Risk comes from not knowing what you are doing, and concentrated not-knowing is the fastest path to permanent loss that exists in this market.

That is why this chapter sits in the middle of the book and not at the start. The chapters behind you built the foundation. The chapters ahead (statements, valuation, projections, the research funnel) are the engineering that makes a conviction position an investment instead of a wager. A five percent starter position requires an afternoon of work. A thirty percent pillar requires that you know the business the way its CFO knows it. The depth of research must always match the weight of the position. Always.

One refinement to that scale: companies themselves differ in complexity, and the work must be sized to the company as well as the position. A world-famous, heavily documented business (Meta, Google, Netflix, Apple) might cost a competent investor a day or two of serious work to understand well. A smaller, younger, unproven growth company is a different animal entirely: the very kind of position that can grow tenfold demands a full week or more of genuine research before confidence is honest rather than borrowed. The multiplication is simple: position size times company complexity equals required work. Every shortcut taken on that equation is eventually invoiced.

Buffett was right. Diversification is protection against ignorance.

So do not diversify your portfolio. Diversify your enemies, own so few businesses, and know them so deeply, that ignorance has nowhere left to hide.

Seven to twelve companies. The best in the world. Studied without mercy. Held without apology.

Structure designed to bear the load.

Part II, Chapter 8

The War Chest

"Opportunities come infrequently. When it rains gold, put out the bucket, not the thimble."

- Warren Buffett

The War Chest

Every investor eventually meets Mr. Market, so let me introduce you properly.

Benjamin Graham invented him decades ago: a manic business partner who shows up every single day offering to buy your shares or sell you his, at a price that reflects nothing but his mood. One day he tries to sell you a plucked chicken for a fortune. The next day he offers you roasted ribs for a dime.

Most investors spend their lives being infected by his moods. The professional learns to do something else entirely, ignore him for years at a time, and then, on the few days he loses his mind completely, take everything he is willing to give away.

But there is a catch, and the catch is the subject of this chapter. On the day Mr. Market offers ribs for a dime, wanting it buys nothing. Insight buys nothing. Only cash buys.

Cash Is Not a Position. It Is a Weapon.

The standard objection to holding cash is mathematically correct and strategically blind.

Cash earns nothing, the argument goes. Every dollar sitting idle is a dollar not compounding. Over long periods the market rises, so time out of the market is a guaranteed drag. All true. And all of it prices cash as an asset, which is the mistake.

Cash is not an asset in your portfolio. Cash is an option on everyone else's panic, an option with no expiration date, as Seth Klarman calls it. His firm has famously held twenty or even thirty percent in cash for years at a time while critics called it lazy. David Tepper sat frozen in cash until March 2009, then bought the banks the world was certain were dying, and made billions on the recovery. Stanley Druckenmiller could swing from fully invested to flat in a week, and then sit, sometimes for months, doing nothing at all.

These men did not hold cash out of fear. They held it out of preparation. The market reliably manufactures moments of irrational pricing, every few years, without fail, since the beginning of markets. Those moments are where decades of returns get compressed into months. And they are only available to investors who arrive with two things: conviction and cash. Conviction tells you what to buy. Cash lets you buy it.

The Doctrine

Here is the system I have run since my early years, in full.

I hold ten to twenty percent of my total capital in cash. The war chest. It does not sit inside my brokerage account, and this detail matters more than it sounds. It lives in a separate account entirely, out of sight of the buy button. Money adjacent to a trading screen gets spent on Tuesday-afternoon temptations. Money in a separate room gets spent on generational opportunities, because moving it requires a deliberate act. The friction is the feature. An architect does not store the emergency reserves on the construction site.

> *The war chest fills during ordinary times, from income and from discipline. And it is spent according to one rule: it deploys when there is blood in the streets, and only then. Not on dips. Not on a stock going ten percent on sale. It waits for the moments when the market is pricing the end of the world – because the world, so far, has stubbornly refused to end.*

In eight and a half years, I have emptied the war chest to zero exactly twice.

March 2020.

COVID crashed the global market thirty percent in weeks. Half the world believed the economy was finished; the other half was too scared to act. We knew something simpler: the world would keep spinning, and the great companies would come out the other side stronger. So while our existing positions bled, and they bled badly, we went hunting. Every dollar of reserve went into wonderful businesses that were only cheap because of a mood. By year-end, several of those purchases had doubled, and the portfolio finished 2020 more than four times larger than it began.

The 2022 bear market.

A different beast, not a crash but a grind, twelve slow months of decline. My portfolio fell fifty-five percent from its peak. And through that entire year, the war chest drained, month after month, into my highest-conviction positions at prices we may never see again. You read the Palantir table in the previous chapter, 1,440 shares in December 2021 became 9,600 by December 2022, most of them bought with reserves built in calmer years. The chest hit zero near the bottom. Not exact, just a bit before, two months I had to simply watch. The two years that followed were the best of my life: plus 131%, then plus 203%.

- Twice deployed.
- Twice to zero.

Both times into maximum fear. That is the entire design.

Understand that this means I am always investing in two modes at once. Mode one is the empire: a fixed amount, every month, brick by brick, contribution by contribution, into the positions I already believe in. Unglamorous and unstoppable.

Mode two is the war chest deployment, and it is a different animal entirely: opportunistic, patient for months and then feral. When the moment comes and the whole market breaks, or one of my highest-conviction companies goes on sale, I will suddenly drop thirty, fifty, a hundred thousand dollars into a single name in a week. Brick by brick, and then, occasionally, by the truckload. Chapter 9 gives this second mode its proper name.

The Doctrine, Measured

Most investing doctrines cannot be measured. This one can, and the measurement is my favorite pair of numbers in this book.

My portfolio's time-weighted return (what one dollar invested at the start compounded into, ignoring the timing of my deposits) is 24.2% per year. That number measures stock selection. Call it the skill metric.

My money-weighted return (the return on my actual dollars, weighted by when they entered) is over 50% per year.

Stop and look at the distance between those numbers, because that gap is the war chest, expressed in arithmetic. The same stocks, the same decisions about what to own, produced twice the return on my actual capital, purely because of when the capital arrived. The heaviest deployments of my life landed in the spring of 2020 and the depths of 2022, immediately before the two strongest runs the portfolio ever produced. Selection built the first twenty-four points. Timing courage built the rest.

I want to be precise about what I am claiming, because this is not market timing. I did not predict the COVID crash. I did not forecast the 2022 bear. I have never correctly predicted anything macroeconomic in my life, and neither has anyone else you follow. The war chest requires zero prediction. It requires preparation: holding the reserve through the boring years, which is genuinely hard. And then recognition, which is easy, because the moments of blood are never subtle. You will not need an indicator to spot them. The headlines will be screaming, your portfolio will be deep red, and everyone you know will be selling.

> *That is the moment the system was built for. Prediction is impossible. Preparation is merely uncomfortable. The entire edge lives in that difference.*

The Hard Part Nobody Warns You About

The mechanics of the war chest take one paragraph to learn. The psychology takes years, and it attacks from two directions.

In bull markets, the reserve humiliates you. Every month, your idle fifteen percent visibly underperforms your friends who are fully invested in whatever is flying. This lasts for years, not weeks. 2023, 2024, 2025 – the market ran, and a disciplined reserve spent those years looking like a mistake. It was not a mistake. It was a premium being paid for an insurance policy that pays out at the precise moment everything else fails.

> *Every bull market sows its own destruction; the chest exists for the harvest.*

In crashes, it terrifies you. The theory says buy when there is blood in the streets. The reality is that when the moment arrives, the blood is yours, and bleeding out is real possibility. In March 2020 my existing positions were down catastrophically while I was wiring in reserves. In 2022 I deployed into a portfolio that had been falling for eleven consecutive months. Buying at the bottom sounds heroic in books. In real time it feels like reinforcing a burning building, and every voice around you, plus several inside you, says stop.

This is why the war chest cannot be improvised. The decision to deploy cannot be made during the crisis, because during the crisis you will be the least rational you have ever been. The decision is made now, in calm, and written down: the reserve exists for broad, indiscriminate panic; it deploys in stages into the highest-conviction names on the watch list; it goes to zero only when the opportunity is generational. Then, when the sirens start, there is no decision left to make. Only execution of drawings that were finished long before the storm.

> *Panic is a transfer of assets to the prepared. The war chest is how you register on the receiving side.*

One boundary completes the doctrine, and it points the other way: there is such a thing as too much cash. The war chest is ten to twenty percent. Not forty, not sixty, never 'mostly cash waiting for the crash.'

Statistically, roughly three out of four years end green; the default winning position in the market is long, and a portfolio hiding in cash is losing the most reliable bet in finance while it waits. Even when the market is flying and bargains are extinct, I keep contributing and let the chest drift toward twenty-five percent at the absolute most. Beyond that line, caution stops being a strategy and becomes a forecast, and Chapter 21 will have words about forecasts.

Rebuilding

One final rule completes the system: the chest refills.

After 2020, I rebuilt the reserve while the market recovered. After 2022, I rebuilt it again. Today it stands at roughly $400,000, a bit over ten percent of total capital, sitting in its separate account, and not idle, either. The chest lives in Treasury bills, laddered in monthly steps – one, three, six months out, like ammunition stacked in the trenches, waiting patiently for Mr. Market's next breakdown. It might wait three years. It might wait three months. The waiting is not a cost. The waiting is the strategy.

Because the pattern of markets is the most reliable thing about them. Euphoria, complacency, panic, despair, recovery. The wheel has turned this way for a century and it is not stopping for us. Somewhere ahead, with total certainty, is another March 2020. Another 2022. Another day when magnificent businesses trade for a dime because the crowd needs liquidity and has run out of courage.

On that day, most investors will discover they are spectators.

You will be a buyer. The chest is already filling.

The Reserve Cycle

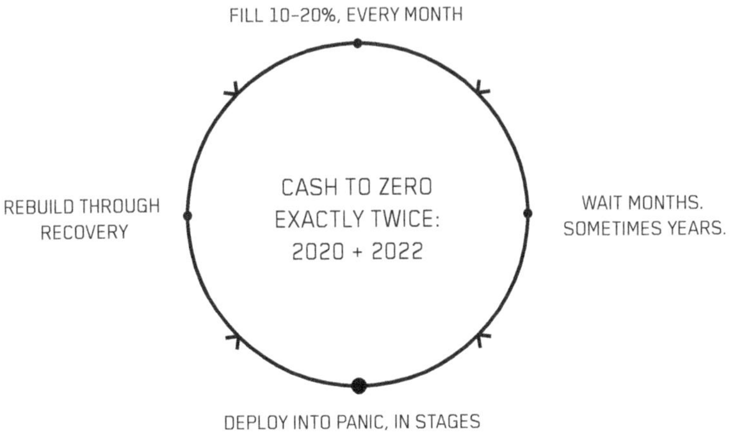

Part II, Chapter 9

Position Sizing: Pouring Concrete in Stages

"Soros has taught me that when you have tremendous conviction on a trade, you have to go for the jugular. It takes courage to be a pig. It takes courage to ride a profit with huge leverage."

-Stanley Druckenmiller

Position Sizing: Pouring Concrete in Stages

Chapter 7 told you how many companies to own. This chapter answers the harder operational question: how much of each, and how you get there.

Because here is what the Palantir table in Chapter 7 demonstrated, and what most readers miss on first pass: I did not buy a conviction position. I built one: a single position growing from 160 shares to 640, to 1,440, and eventually to 9,600 and beyond. Three years, in more than twenty separate purchases, as evidence accumulated. Nobody pours a foundation in one truckload. Concrete goes in stages, and each layer sets before the next arrives.

Starter, Building, Built

Every position in a disciplined portfolio exists in one of three states, and the rules differ for each.

- **The starter position** – one to three percent of the portfolio. This is a stake in the ground, placed when research is promising but incomplete. Its function is attention. Money in a company changes how you read about it. You notice the earnings, you hear the conference calls differently, you do the work you would otherwise postpone forever. A starter position is tuition for the deep research phase.

- **The building position** – three to ten percent, growing in deliberate increments as two things rise together: your knowledge and the evidence. Every addition should be justified by something new, a quarter that confirmed the thesis, a 10-K read cover to cover, a margin inflection arriving on schedule. You are matching capital to conviction, and conviction is only allowed to grow at the speed of evidence. If the price falls while the evidence improves, additions accelerate; that was 2022. There is a precise logic behind that acceleration: if my research said the business was attractive at fifteen dollars, then at ten, with operations intact, it is not more frightening, it is objectively better. The price fell; the risk fell with it, because every dollar now buys more margin of safety. This is why doubling down as the price sinks is rational exactly when, and only when, the operational performance is rock solid, and why the entire method depends on knowing the operations well enough to certify that. If the price rises while the evidence stalls, additions stop, no matter how good momentum feels.

- **The built position** – ten to twenty percent, and twenty is the ceiling for new capital. I will not deploy fresh money into a position beyond a fifth of the portfolio, no matter how good it feels. What appreciation does afterward is a different matter entirely: if the stock itself grows the position to thirty, forty, fifty percent while the thesis keeps verifying, that concentration was earned by the company, not wagered by me, and Chapter 7 already explained why I let it stand.

The discipline binding all three stages together is one sentence: the depth of research must always match the weight of the position. An afternoon of work licenses a starter. Only mastery licenses a pillar.

The Written Plan

Now the rule that separates professionals from the perpetually improvising: the scaling plan is written before the first purchase.

Before I open any position, one page exists. What the company is and why it wins. What position size the current evidence justifies. What specific developments would justify each next tranche. What price zones I consider attractive for additions. And, most important, what would falsify the thesis and trigger an exit.

The page takes thirty minutes and it is worth more than any valuation model in this book, for one reason: it is written by the calm version of you, and executed by whichever version of you exists on the day the stock is down forty percent. The calm version makes better decisions. The written plan is how the calm version stays in charge, so that when the storm arrives there is nothing left to decide. Only to execute.

Without the page, every red day reopens every question, and you will renegotiate your conviction with yourself at exactly the moments you are least qualified to do so.

And beneath that page sits the machinery that makes it honest: a fully built projection model – my own numbers, from my own research, telling me what is reasonable and probable.

Not merely possible; probable. The price zones on the plan are not borrowed price targets from someone's video, they fall out of the model. This is the difference between a plan and a wish, and Chapter 19 builds the machine in full.

The Portfolio as a Machine

Zoom out from single positions and the whole structure has a shape. Three functional layers:

- **Core** – 60 to 80 percent. The pillars. High-conviction, deeply understood, long-horizon holdings. This layer generates the wealth, and it changes rarely. Each position enters or leaves the core perhaps once a year, often less.

- **Opportunistic** – 10 to 30 percent. Asymmetric ideas earlier in their evidence curve – the starter and building positions, the recent-IPO candidates of Chapter 22, the companies where the thesis is forming. Sized smaller precisely because they are riskier; this layer feeds the core with tomorrow's pillars, and its failures are designed to be affordable.
- **Cash** – 10 to 20 percent. The war chest of Chapter 8. It waits.

Every part of the machine has a function. Some parts generate. Some protect. Some wait. Your task is calibrating the proportions to your temperament – tight enough to outperform, loose enough that you never crack in the parts of the cycle that punish conviction.

Building the Empire vs. Going for the Jugular

One final distinction, borrowed from Stanley Druckenmiller, completes the sizing doctrine: "When you find a great trade, you have to go for the jugular."

> *There are two modes of deploying capital, and both are correct – at different times. Ninety percent of your investing life is empire mode: steady, unglamorous, contribution-by-contribution additions to quality positions at reasonable prices. This mode built the base of every fortune, and it never makes anyone feel like a genius.*

And then, a few times per decade, the market hands you a jugular moment: a great business, priced for extinction, for reasons you have verified are mood rather than structure.

Palantir at seven dollars was one. The COVID bottom was another. In those moments, the empire rules suspend. You size aggressively, deploy the reserve, and act with a violence of conviction that would be reckless on any ordinary Tuesday.

One correctly seized jugular moment can outperform five years of empire mode; you read the arithmetic of mine in Chapter 8.

The skill is knowing which mode the market is offering, and never confusing an ordinary Tuesday for a jugular moment just because you are bored.

Size follows evidence. Evidence follows work. And the plan is written before the money moves.

That is how a foundation gets poured: in stages, on schedule, from drawings.

Part II, Chapter 10

Moats: Survival of the Fittest

"Competition is for losers."

- Peter Thiel

Moats: Survival of the Fittest

Two companies grow revenue at the same rate for three years. One compounds shareholder wealth for the next two decades. The other slowly rots while its investors wait for a recovery that never comes.

The difference is almost never visible in the growth numbers. It lives in a question the income statement cannot answer: what happens when serious competitors show up? Because they will show up. High profits are a beacon; every profitable niche in a market economy attracts capital, imitation, and price wars.

Pause on that mechanism before we learn to defend against it, because it is both ruthless and beautiful. This is Darwinism running in markets.

The same principle that shaped every living thing now shaping every business: variation, competition, survival of the fittest. It looks like waste from up close, all those failed challengers and burned capital. Step back and it is the engine of everything good about the modern world: the best offering wins, the consumer wins, and humanity gets better products at lower prices, forever, without anyone commanding it.

Nature and the market run the same operating system. Your job as an investor is simply to own the organisms that keep winning the selection.

> *The default fate of every good business is to have its margins competed away.*

A moat is whatever stops that from happening. It is the structural property that lets a business earn superior returns year after year while competitors visibly try, and visibly fail, to take them. Buffett organized his whole career around this idea, and this book treats it as a non-negotiable: no moat, no position. A great price on a moatless business is a discount on a melting ice cube.

The Seven

Moats come in a handful of recognizable species. Learn to name them on sight.

- **Network effects.** The product becomes more valuable as more people use it, which means the leader's advantage compounds automatically. Meta is the canonical case: every user makes the platform more valuable to every other user, and a competitor cannot offer "the same product with fewer people" because fewer people is a worse product. Network-effect businesses tend toward winner-take-most outcomes – which is precisely why we want to own the number one player, not the challenger.

- **Switching costs.** Leaving the product is expensive or dangerous for the customer. Palantir is my portfolio's example: once its software is woven into an organization's operations (data pipelines built, workflows rewired, staff trained) ripping it out is a multi-year project with existential risk. Customers stay because leaving is worse than staying. Revenue with high switching costs behaves less like sales and more like an annuity.

- **Brand.** The test of a brand moat is whether customers pay more, or reflexively choose the product, because of what the name guarantees. And note the sophisticated variant: Costco's brand is trust-based rather than premium – the name stands for "you are not being ripped off." Costco has enormous pricing power and deliberately declines to use it, passing savings to members to deepen loyalty and volume. Pricing power held in reserve is still a moat. Sometimes the deepest one.

- **Cost advantage.** The business produces what competitors produce, structurally cheaper, through scale, process, logistics, or vertical integration – and can therefore either undercut rivals or out-earn them at the same price. This is the other half of the Costco machine: extreme operating efficiency, limited SKUs, rapid inventory turnover, supplier leverage. A cost advantage rooted in structure is durable; one rooted in temporarily cheap inputs is not.

- **Process power.** The rarest to see and the hardest to copy: a company whose advantage is the way the entire organization operates. Hundreds or thousands of interlocking routines, decisions, incentives, habits, and cultural norms, compounded over years into a system that consistently produces better results. The cruel part for competitors is that everything is visible and nothing is replicable: they can see what the company does, and still cannot reproduce how the whole organism does it. Toyota's production system was documented for decades and remained unmatched, because the moat was never in the documents. When you find a business whose excellence has no single explanation, you may be looking at the deepest moat of all.

- **Scale and distribution.** The advantage of already being everywhere: fixed costs spread across enormous volume, distribution the challenger must rebuild from zero, data accumulated over decades. Often this wall reinforces the others rather than standing alone. AMD's position rests on engineering, but its ecosystem relationships and manufacturing access are moats a startup cannot conjure with any amount of funding.

- **Proprietary data.** The newest moat, and one growing more valuable by the year: a company that owns, or continuously generates, data competitors cannot access, recreate, or purchase – and whose product or economics materially improve because of it. Every transaction, every sensor reading, every workflow inside the moat feeds a resource no rival can buy at any price. The rise of large language models has sharpened this moat dramatically: the models themselves train on public data and are becoming commodities, which means the differentiated value migrates to whoever can point that intelligence at private data. A company sitting on a decade of proprietary operational data in the age of AI is sitting on refinery-grade crude in the age of the automobile.

Most great businesses stack several moats. Each additional moat multiplies the difficulty for attackers, because they must breach all of them at once.

Moats Move

Here is the intermediate-level truth that separates moat analysis from moat trivia: a moat is not a fact about a company. It is a trajectory. Every moat, every day, is either deepening or eroding. There is no steady state, and your job as an owner is to know which way yours is moving.

A great business compounds its advantages over time. It builds deeper switching costs, a stronger brand, a bigger network with every year of operation, so that the same company becomes progressively harder to attack.

A mediocre business does the reverse, often invisibly at first: the brand coasts on past reputation while the product slips; the technology lead narrows a release at a time; customers stay from inertia and begin evaluating alternatives. The income statement keeps looking fine for years after the wall has cracked. Revenue is a lagging indicator of moat health, which is why investors who watch only financials get blindsided by declines that were structurally visible long before.

So the monitoring questions, asked of every holding, every year:

- Is pricing power being exercised or lost?
- Is customer retention rising or slipping?
- Are challengers gaining share anywhere, even at the low end?
- Is the company reinvesting in the moat (R&D, network, cost structure) or harvesting it?

Recessions are the great moat X-ray: the best businesses tighten their grip in downturns, taking share from weaker rivals while everyone else retreats. Watch who exits a recession stronger. That list is the moat list.

The Afternoon Test

You do not need a consulting engagement to assess a moat. One honest afternoon answers three questions:

1. The Buffett test: if a brilliant, hostile competitor

were handed one billion dollars and five years to destroy this company, how would they do it? If you cannot construct a plausible attack, you have found a wall. If the attack writes itself, so will the ending.

2. Why do customers stay? Not the investor-relations answer. The real one, findable in customer forums, employee reviews, churn numbers. "Because leaving is a nightmare" and "because nothing else has everyone on it" are moats. "Because they have not gotten around to switching" is a countdown.

3. What has happened to prices and margins over five years? A company that raises prices and keeps its customers has proven its moat empirically. A company that only wins on discounts has proven the opposite.

Buy the moat, not the war story. Growth attracts competitors; moats repel them, and in the long run, every return you will ever compound is downstream of a moat someone cannot breach.

Part II, Chapter 11

Management: The General Contractor

"Don't tell me what you think, tell me what you have in your portfolio."

- Nassim Taleb

Management: The General Contractor

When you buy a stock, you are not only buying assets and a moat. You are hiring a management team, handing your capital to specific human beings and outsourcing every decision that will determine its fate for the next decade. You will not sit in their meetings. You cannot overrule their acquisitions. Your only powers are the two you exercise from outside: judging them accurately, and leaving if the judgment turns.

This chapter is about exercising the first power well, so you rarely need the second. Because as an owner, you are, in a very real sense, above the CEO. They work with your capital. Act like it.

Founders or Mercenaries?

Start with the strongest single signal in management analysis: who is running the company, and what do they have at stake?

> *Founder-led companies are structurally different animals, and my portfolio is deliberately full of them – Palantir under Karp, Tesla under Musk, Hims & Hers under Dudum, Meta under Zuckerberg. The pattern is not sentimental. A founder with a controlling stake and a life's mission thinks in decades because the company is not a job to them; it is their calling. They will torch a quarter to win a decade, absorb ridicule through the unprofitable years, and make the aggressive long-term investments that a hired CEO, whose personal horizon is a four-year contract, is structurally punished for making.*

The general form of the signal is skin in the game. How much of the company does leadership own. Not options granted last year, but wealth genuinely at risk alongside yours? Are insiders buying with their own money, or selling into every rally? Perfect alignment is rare; large, held, personal ownership is the closest proxy the outside world gets.

And when the founder is a hired professional instead, the bar simply rises: now the track record and the incentives must do all the work that ownership would have done.

Incentives Tell the Truth

The mission statement sounds good. The annual letter sounds good. Everything a company says about itself sounds good, because saying good things is free. Incentives are where the truth is kept, because incentives cost money.

Open the proxy statement (the one filing almost nobody reads) and find what the executives are paid for. If bonuses vest on this year's stock price or adjusted-EBITDA targets, expect exactly what is being purchased: short-term games, aggressive accounting at the margins, buybacks timed for optics. If compensation vests on multi-year free cash flow growth, per-share value creation, and returns on capital, expect behavior aimed at those things instead. Executives are not villains or heroes. They are rational responders to their own scoreboard, and the proxy statement shows you the scoreboard.

Charlie Munger compressed the entire discipline into nine words: 'Show me the incentive and I will show you the outcome.' The proxy statement is where the incentive is written down. Everything that follows in the company's behavior is the outcome, arriving on schedule.

Fifteen minutes in that document tells you more about the next five years than a hundred interviews.

The Promises Ledger

Talk is graded on a delay, and most investors never go back to grade it. You will.

The method is simple. Take the earnings calls and shareholder letters from three years ago, all public, all free, and write down what management promised: the margin targets, the product timelines, the expansion plans, the "we expect by 2025" sentences. Then hold the list against what happened.

Some teams show a pattern of promising conservatively and delivering early. Palantir's margin expansion arrived on the schedule management described while the stock was being ridiculed at eight dollars – that consistency, quarter after quarter through 2022, was a large part of what let me keep buying. Other teams show the opposite fingerprint: a rolling horizon of profitability "next year," strategic pivots that bury last year's pivot, guidance walked down mid-year, every year. Both patterns are extremely persistent. Teams that deliver keep delivering; teams that promise keep promising.

Three years of receipts beats any impression formed in a single quarter.

Listening to a Call Properly

The earnings call is the one place you regularly hear management think, and most listeners extract nothing from it because they listen for the numbers, which they could have read in the release, instead of the behavior.

Skip to the Q&A; the prepared remarks are theater. Then listen for how questions are handled. Great operators answer the hard question directly, quantify their answers, name their own mistakes unprompted, and say "we do not know yet" when they do not know – the single most credibility-building sentence in corporate life. Warning signs are just as audible: the hard question deflected with vision language, blame consistently located outside the company (macro, weather, "industry headwinds" that somehow spare competitors), buzzwords swelling as specifics shrink, and a new strategic narrative every few quarters.

You are listening for information behind information. You are listening for character under mild pressure. The same character will later operate under severe pressure, with your capital.

The Standard

One more thing management must prove, and it is the subject of a full chapter later: what they do with the profits. Capital allocation, the choice to reinvest, acquire, buy back, or pay out, is where mediocre stewards destroy what great operators build, and Chapter 20 gives it the treatment it deserves.

For now, the hiring standard in one paragraph. Meaningful personal ownership, ideally a founder. Incentives that pay for long-term per-share value, not this quarter's optics. A three-year promise ledger that shows delivery. Direct answers under questioning. And a visible record of treating shareholders' money with more care than their own.

Teams meeting that standard are rare, which is fine, because Chapter 7 already established you only need seven to twelve companies in a lifetime cohort.

Bet on jockeys who own the horse. Everyone else is riding your money for a salary.

Part II, Chapter 12

Supertrends: Building Where the City Grows

"The more we have developed in the past, the more new things will be possible to create in the future."

- Lars Tvede

Supertrends: Building Where the City Grows

Two architects receive identical budgets. One builds a masterpiece in a dying town. The other builds a merely good building in a city doubling every decade.

Twenty years later, nobody remembers the masterpiece.

Location is the variable that forgives sins and punishes perfection, and it has an exact analogue in investing: the structural direction of the world. A well-run company in a shrinking industry is swimming against a current that never tires. An imperfect company inside a decade-long structural shift gets pushed forward by forces larger than any quarterly stumble. Before you study a single balance sheet, ask the location question: is this business built where the city is growing?

Trends and Supertrends

First, a hard distinction, because the failure mode of this chapter is deadly, and it is called chasing hype.

- A trend is a story the market is excited about. It lives on magazine covers, produces vertical stock charts, and dies within a few years, taking late arrivals' capital with it. Trendy stocks in trendy industries are candles that burn fast and burn out; the meme cycles, the SPAC waves, the quantum-computing manias. The graveyard of retail portfolios is landscaped with them.
- A supertrend is a structural rearrangement of how the world works, unfolding over decades, visible in boring data rather than headlines: software absorbing every industry's operations; artificial intelligence becoming a production input

like electricity; healthcare shifting from institutions to direct, personalized, digital delivery; finance migrating out of branches and into software. Supertrends do not need your belief. They grind forward through recessions, elections, and sentiment cycles alike, because they are driven by economics and demographics, not enthusiasm.

The test between them: a trend needs the story to continue. A supertrend continues whether or not anyone tells the story. If removing the excitement removes the growth, you are looking at a candle.

The Portfolio as a Map of the Future

Look back at the current portfolio in Appendix B and you will find it is a set of coordinates – each position an intersection of a great company and a supertrend with a decade of runway.

Palantir and AMD sit on the largest structural shift of our lifetime: intelligence becoming infrastructure, one selling the software layer where AI meets institutional decision-making, the other selling the silicon it runs on. Hims & Hers sits on healthcare's migration to direct digital delivery – a distribution revolution in the largest spending category of human life. SoFi rides banking's generational move into software. Tesla spans the electrification of transport and the automation of labor. Meta owns human digital attention and the network effects beneath it.

Seven positions, four or five tectonic plates. That is deliberate. When you hold only seven to twelve companies, each one must answer not only "is this a great business?" but "is this a great business standing where the next decade is being built?" Concentration makes location non-negotiable: you do not have enough slots to spend one on a masterpiece in a dying town.

Own the future. The past is fully priced.

Why America

One location decision sits above the industry level, and I will state my position because it is contrarian to standard advice: the overwhelming majority of my capital is in United States companies, on purpose, permanently.

> *Standard doctrine says diversify globally. But examine what the doctrine buys. The US market offers a century of legal tradition protecting shareholders, the deepest liquidity on earth, disclosure standards that make the analysis in this book possible – and it is where the pinnacle of innovation concentrates.*

The supertrends of this chapter are being built disproportionately in one country: the AI stack, the software giants, the platforms. Capital, talent, and ambition flow there in a self-reinforcing loop decades old, like a civilization pursuing the science victory while others fight over the map.

Diversifying away from that, in the name of geography, is very often diversification into weakness – trading the best jurisdiction and the best companies for exposure to markets with thinner protections, slower growth, and no seat at the technological frontier. I do not need my portfolio to be a map of the world. I need it to be a map of where the future is being manufactured.

William Gibson said it best: the future is already here; it is just not evenly distributed. That is the entire geographic thesis in one sentence. The future is not built everywhere at once; it is driven by a startlingly small number of companies and individuals, clustered in a few places. Most of the world's economic activity is people doing what has been done for decades or centuries. A restaurant today operates much as one did in 1950. Meanwhile a few thousand people building frontier AI models are moving the whole species forward. A portfolio is a claim on the future; it should be pointed at the places where the future is unevenly piled up.

This is a judgment, not a law of physics, and it deserves re-examination every few years. It has been correct for the entire investing lifetime of everyone reading this book.

Riding a Supertrend Without Overpaying

A final discipline, because supertrends have a cruel property: everyone eventually notices them, and by then the obvious beneficiaries trade at prices that assume the future twice over.

Three rules keep the location edge without paying the tourist price.

1. **The supertrend is a filter, never a thesis.** "AI is big" justified nothing; the company still needs the moat of Chapter 10, the management of Chapter 11, and a price defensible in Part III.

2. **Prefer the toll roads.** Businesses that collect from a supertrend's traffic regardless of which participant wins are safer than bets on any single winner.

3. **Exploit the market's rhythm.** Even genuine supertrends move in waves of hype and disillusionment, and the disillusionment phases (Palantir 2022, the post-IPO deserts of Chapter 22) are when decade-long structural growth goes

on clearance. The supertrend tells you what street to stand on. Valuation tells you when to buy the building.

The next decade is already under construction, in plain sight, in the boring data.

Do not buy where the city was. Buy where the cranes are, and then hold while the skyline fills in around you.

Part II, Chapter 13

99 No's, 1 Hell Yes

"The person that turns over the most rocks wins the game."

- Peter Lynch

99 No's, 1 Hell Yes

There are more than six thousand publicly traded companies in the United States alone. You will own seven to twelve.

Sit with that ratio for a moment, because it defines the actual job. Out there is every kind of company: a few great ones, many merely good, and a vast majority you should reject on sight. Finding the good ones is no achievement, they are obvious, and anyone can name twenty. The skill is saying no: quickly, to the many that fail early, and reluctantly, to the good ones that are simply not great, until your capital ends up in only the handful that survive every gate.

> *This skill has an old-fashioned name that our culture has turned into an insult: judgment. The ability to rank (this is better than that) and to act on the ranking. Reclaim the word. It is the entire profession.*

This chapter is the funnel that turns six thousand into seven, without consuming your life.

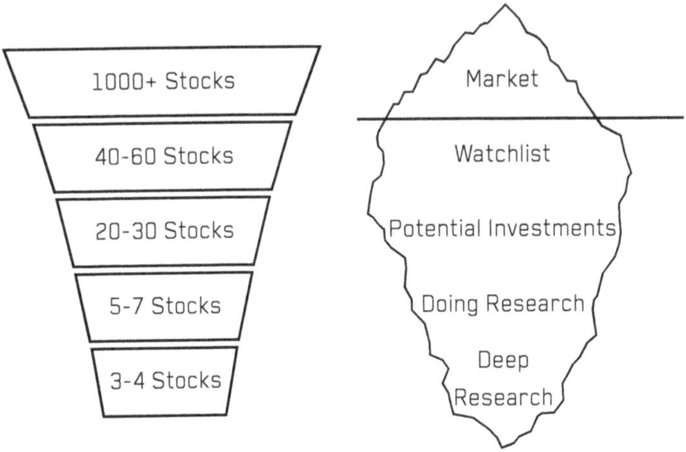

Stage Zero: The Whole Market to The Watch List

You cannot research six thousand companies, and you do not need to. The first cut costs almost nothing, because you make it with knowledge you already have.

Keep a standing watch list of forty to sixty companies, businesses you are roughly familiar with, understand the basic model of, and would consider owning at some price. It assembles itself from ordinary life as a market participant: the giants everyone knows, the products you and people around you use, the names surfacing repeatedly from sources you respect, the recent IPOs of Chapter 22 consolidating toward their moment. Entry standards are loose but real: a plausible moat, a supertrend location, revenue that exists. Speculative lottery tickets do not make the list, no matter how exciting the story.

The watch list is a garden, not a museum: names enter as they prove themselves interesting, exit as theses die, and sit for years, watched casually through earnings seasons, until something changes. That "something" is usually one of two events: the fundamentals inflect, or the price collapses while the fundamentals hold. Either one promotes a company to Stage One.

Stage One: Qualitative – Is This a Great Business?

A few hours per company, big picture only, in the exact order of Chapter 10 through 12: What does it sell and why do customers stay? Is there a moat? Who runs it and what do they have at stake? Is it standing where the city grows?

No spreadsheets yet. Numbers answer "how well is it going?" – a pointless question until you have answered "is this worth going well?" Most candidates die right here, killed by an honest paragraph: the moat is imaginary, the industry is a candle, the management page reads like a casino.

Good. Every early no is hours of quantitative work you never have to do. You are not paid for research. You are paid for outcomes, and the funnel's efficiency is a return on your scarcest asset, attention.

Stage Two: Quantitative – Do the Numbers Confirm the Story?

Survivors get the financial statements: the income statement's story (Chapter 14), the balance sheet and cash flow truth serum (Chapter 15), margins and their trajectory (Chapter 16), and, for the serious few, the 10-K, read efficiently (Chapter 17). One question drives it all: does the arithmetic confirm the narrative from Stage One? A "network effects" story should show up as pricing power and retention in the numbers. A "great management" story should show up as returns on capital. When story and statements disagree, the statements are telling the truth, and the company exits the funnel.

Red flag protocol at every stage: one genuine red flag (deteriorating cash quality, serial dilution, incentives pointed the wrong way) and you simply stop. There are six thousand other companies; you owe this one nothing.

Stage Three: Projections – What Is It Worth, and What Could Go Wrong?

Only the finalists, a handful per year, earn the full treatment of Chapters 18 and 19: revenue modeled forward, margins estimated, bull, base, and bear cases, a price range that defines what buying makes sense. Projections come last for the same reason an engineer does not calculate loads for a building that failed the site survey. By the time you build the model, you should already believe; the model's job is to tell you the price at which belief becomes an investment, and a starter position (Chapter 9) opens the ownership clock.

The Yield

Now calibrate your expectations, because the funnel's honest arithmetic surprises people.

For every ten to fifteen companies you take through serious research, expect one or two to genuinely, pleasantly surprise you – businesses whose quality is not yet fully recognized in the price. That is the hit rate of a working process, not a failing one. Which means a year in which you deeply research fifteen companies and buy one is a successful year. The other fourteen were not wasted: they built the pattern library that makes your next fifteen faster, and they populated the watch list with companies you now genuinely understand, waiting for their 2022.

> *This is also why the funnel and the war chest are one system. The funnel produces conviction. The chest produces capacity. When the market breaks, you are not "looking for opportunities" – you are executing a shopping list written years earlier, at prices you never expected to see.*

And this is where empire mode meets the jugular. Most purchases are routine, the funnel's steady output, added to steadily. But every few years, the funnel and the panic align on the same name, and that alignment is the moment everything in this book exists for. You will not need to be told when it happens. You will recognize it, because you will have already done the work, years earlier, in calm, on a company everyone has just decided to hate.

Say no ninety-nine times. Opportunities are everywhere, but your attention is finite. Use it with intent.

The one hell yes will pay for every no you ever said.

PART III: THE STRUCTURE

Part III, Chapter 14

Every Income Statement Tells a Story

"It is a capital mistake to theorize before one has data."

- Arthur Conan Doyle.

Every Income Statement Tells a Story

Part III begins here, with the engineering. And it begins with a promise: the financial statements are not math. They are language, the native language of business, and like any language, they stop being intimidating the moment you stop decoding words and start hearing sentences.

The income statement is where you learn to hear. It is the quarterly narrative of a business: what came in, what it cost, and what survived the journey to the bottom. Most investors read it like a phone book, scanning for one number – did earnings beat?

You are going to read it like a story, top to bottom, and the story is almost never in the numbers themselves. It is in the relationships between them.

The Waterfall

Every income statement is the same waterfall, and money can only flow down it:

Revenue, everything customers paid. Then cost of revenue comes out, leaving gross profit: what the product itself earns. Then operating expenses (R&D, sales, administration, the cost of running the machine), leaving operating income: what the business earns. Then interest, taxes, and the miscellaneous, leaving net income, which divided by the share count becomes earnings per share: what you, the owner, earned.

Each level of the waterfall answers a different question.

Revenue asks: is anyone buying? Gross profit asks: is the product itself economically sound? Operating income asks: is the machine well run? Net income asks: what reaches the owners? A company can succeed at the top of the waterfall and die in the middle (plenty do) which is why no single line can tell the whole story.

The Golden Relationship

Here is the sentence that upgrades your reading forever: what matters is not how fast each line grows, but how the growth rates relate to each other down the waterfall.

> *The signature of a great business in its prime reads like this: revenue grows, costs grow slower than revenue, so operating income grows faster than revenue, and EPS grows faster still. Each line amplifies the one above it, and that cascade has a name: operating leverage, the single most beautiful pattern in financial statements. It means the machine gets more profitable with scale: every new dollar of sales arrives cheaper than the last, and growth is compounding quality, not just size.*

Two real silhouettes from my own earnings reviews show the pattern and its absence. One defense contractor's quarter: revenue up mid-single digits, unremarkable, but costs nearly flat, so operating profit quadrupled from $500 million to $2 billion. A boring top line hiding an explosive middle; the story was three layers down. Against it, a beloved restaurant chain the same season: revenue up slightly, expenses up faster, operating income shrinking, EPS flat. Two companies "growing revenue." Opposite stories. The waterfall separates them in ninety seconds.

The inverse cascade is the one that should frighten you: revenue growing while operating income grows slower or shrinks. That is a business buying its growth, each new dollar of sales costing more than a dollar to obtain, and it is the most common expensive illusion in growth investing.

THE WATERFALL – AMD, Q1 2026

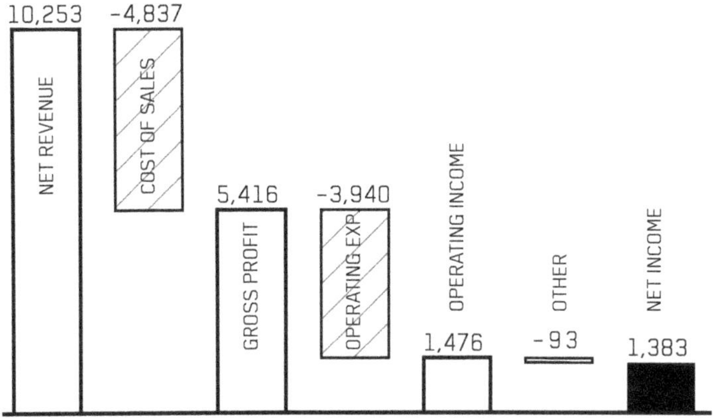

YoY GROWTH, DOWN THE WATERFALL:

+38% → +45% → +83% → +95%

COSTS GREW SLOWER THAN REVENUE – SO EVERY LEVEL GREW FASTER THAN THE ONE ABOVE IT. THIS IS OPERATING LEVERAGE.

Strip the One-Time Items First

One discipline stands between you and constant misreading, and skipping it invalidates everything else: before judging any income statement, remove what does not repeat.

Net income is polluted, routinely, by items that have nothing to do with the operating business: gains or losses on investments the company holds, tax swings and one-off credits, restructuring charges, legal settlements, and the modern classic: non-cash "fair value" movements on stakes in other companies, which can make a mediocre quarter look heroic or a fine quarter look catastrophic. A company can "grow EPS 300%" because it marked up an investment, while the actual business shrank.

So the protocol: read the footnotes below the statement, identify every one-time item, and mentally rebuild the quarter without them. Compare clean against clean. Only then grade. This single habit will put you ahead of most of the people producing headlines about the very same report, because headlines grade the polluted number, always.

The Rest of the Diagnostic

With the statement cleaned, a short checklist completes the read. Share count, always: EPS has two parts, and a company can grow "earnings per share" by shrinking shares (fine, if bought back sensibly) or hide stagnation by printing them (dilution – your slice shrinking inside a growing pie). Gross margin direction across several quarters: expansion signals pricing power compounding; erosion signals a moat under pressure, visible here years before the headlines. The R&D question: cutting research inflates today's operating income by selling the future. Profitable quarters purchased at the cost of the decade. And one quarter is weather; the story only counts as climate across four to eight of them, read in sequence.

The Grade

At the end of every read, force a verdict, a letter grade, A through F, written down. The letter grade is arbitrary; the forcing is the point: a grade demands you weigh the whole waterfall, the cleaned numbers, the trajectory, and commit. An A is the full cascade: clean acceleration down the waterfall, margins expanding, share count honest. A C grows the top line while the middle deteriorates. A D shrinks where it matters, and no narrative rescues it.

Do this for your holdings every quarter and for watchlist

candidates in Stage Two of the funnel, and something compounds that has nothing to do with any single company: pattern recognition. After fifty statements, you will read one in five minutes and hear the story before you have consciously parsed a line. That speed is fluency.

The numbers are the vocabulary. The relationships are the grammar.

Learn the grammar, and every quarterly report becomes a public confession.

Part III, Chapter 15

The Structural Inspection: Balance Sheet and Cash Flow

"Only when the tide goes out do you discover who's been swimming naked."

- Warren Buffett

The Structural Inspection: Balance Sheet and Cash Flow

The income statement tells you how the business performed. The other two statements tell you whether it will survive, and whether it is telling the truth.

Think of the trio as an inspection sequence. The income statement is the tour of the finished floors: impressive, and the part every seller wants to show you. The balance sheet is the structural survey: the foundation, the load calculations, what the building owns versus what it owes. And the cash flow statement is the meter in the basement that cannot be repainted, the record of actual money moving. Accounting is the language of business, but like any language it can be used to persuade as well as inform. These two statements are where persuasion goes to die.

Many portfolios have been ruined by companies with beautiful income statements, weak balance sheets, and poor cash flow quality. This chapter makes sure yours is never one of them.

The Balance Sheet: Can It Survive?

The balance sheet is a photograph: one date, everything owned, everything owed, and the difference, which belongs to you. Read it with three questions.

Can it survive a storm? Compare cash and equivalents against total debt, then check the maturity schedule in the footnotes, when the debt comes due.

The spectrum runs from the fortress (billions in cash, zero debt, Palantir through the 2022 collapse, which is precisely why I could keep buying while the price said bankruptcy) to the leveraged shell that dies in the first credit winter.

Debt is not automatically evil; debt that must be refinanced at unknown rates during the exact recessions that crush revenue is how good businesses have their equity handed to creditors. A fortress balance sheet converts recessions from threats into shopping sprees, remember from Chapter 10 that the strongest companies tighten their grip in downturns. That grip is financed here.

What is the equity made of? Not all assets are equally real. Cash is real. Inventory and receivables are probably real, unless they are growing much faster than revenue, a classic early warning that product is piling up unsold or customers are not paying. And a soft spot deserves special attention: goodwill, the accounting residue of past acquisitions. A balance sheet where equity is mostly goodwill is a building whose foundation is mostly paperwork, one impairment announcement from shrinking.

> *Which direction is it moving? Like moats, balance sheets have trajectories. Cash building, debt retiring, equity compounding: a business getting stronger every year it operates. The reverse (debt creeping up to fund operations, equity thinning) is a slow leak that income statements can conceal for years.*

The Cash Flow Statement: Is It Telling the Truth?

Net income is an opinion. It is assembled from estimates, accrual timing, and judgment calls, all within the rules, all somewhat elastic. Cash is a fact. The cash flow statement reconciles the opinion to the fact, and the reconciliation is where fiction gets caught.

The number that matters most in all of financial analysis lives here: free cash flow – cash generated by operations, minus the capital spending required to keep the machine running.

What remains is truth serum: actual surplus money, after everything, available for the capital allocation decisions of Chapter 20.

Great businesses generate free cash flow, year after year, cycle after cycle. Mediocre ones generate promises (revenue, adjusted metrics, "profitability next year") while the cash line stays stubbornly empty. If you cannot see the cash accumulating, it probably is not real.

The single most powerful check in this chapter takes thirty seconds: put net income next to operating cash flow, across several years. They should track each other. A company reporting fat profits while cash flow lags far behind, persistently, is manufacturing earnings the meter cannot see: receivables games, capitalized costs, accrual gymnastics. The income statement can be persuaded. The cash flow statement cannot.

The Financial Engineering Catalog

Certain patterns recur so reliably in the wreckage of retail portfolios that they deserve to be named, memorized, and treated as automatic funnel exits.

- **The debt-fueled dividend.** A company borrowing to sustain a payout it no longer earns, renting the costume of a quality business while hollowing the structure. Check: is free cash flow covering the dividend? If the dividend is financed on the liabilities side, you are being paid with your own building materials.
- **The buyback trap.** Buybacks are wonderful at low prices with surplus cash, and destructive when debt-funded at peak prices to flatter EPS – often, check the proxy from Chapter 11, in the

same years executive bonuses vest on EPS. Same tool, opposite outcomes; the balance sheet tells you which one you are watching.

- **Stealth dilution.** Stock-based compensation that quietly grows the share count a few percent every year: a real cost, conveniently excluded from "adjusted" earnings, paid by you in ownership. Track shares outstanding over five years. The trajectory is the truth.

- **Serial acquisition indigestion.** Growth assembled by buying revenue every year, goodwill swelling, organic growth unknowable, until one impairment charge confesses a decade of overpaying at once.

None of these requires forensic skill to catch. Every one is visible in the two statements of this chapter, usually years before the ending, to the small minority who look.

The complete inspection, then: the income statement for performance, the balance sheet for survival, the cash flow statement for honesty.

Three documents, published quarterly, a standard of disclosure investors a century ago would have considered fantasy. The edge is not access. The edge is that almost nobody reads past the first one.

Profits are the story a company tells. Cash is the story it can pay for.

Part III, Chapter 16

Margins: The Backbone of Great Business Models

"Your margin is my opportunity."

- Jeff Bezos

Margins: The Backbone of Great Business Models

Two companies grow revenue at exactly 25% a year. Five years later, one has multiplied its shareholders' money several times over. The other has gone sideways and broken hearts.

> *Same growth. Radically different outcomes. The difference is almost always margins, and if you want to understand why some businesses compound capital for decades while others constantly disappoint, this chapter is the mechanism. Most investors obsess over revenue growth. Understandable, but incomplete: revenue tells you how big a business is getting. Margins tell you the economic quality and durability of what is getting big.*

Margins measure how much of each dollar of revenue the company keeps. They are, simultaneously, a readout of efficiency, of pricing power, of moat strength, and of resilience in bad times. And critically for the investor: margins are where the future hides. Where a business will be in three years is a function of what its margin profile becomes, which, unlike the future itself, can be reasoned about today.

The Three That Matter

Each margin is a level of the Chapter 14 waterfall, expressed as a percentage of revenue, and each answers a different question.

- **Gross margin** – revenue minus the direct cost of producing what was sold. This is the purest look at the economic strength of the product itself: how profitable is the thing, before any corporate overhead touches it? Software keeping 80 cents of every dollar and a grocer keeping 25 are living in different physical universes, and no amount of management brilliance moves a company from one universe to the other. Gross margin is largely a fact about the business model.

- **Operating margin** – what remains after R&D, sales, and administration. This is where execution and management quality show up: two companies with identical gross margins can run wildly different operating margins depending on how well the machine is managed. Gross margin is the business model; operating margin is the operators.
- **Net margin** – what is left after everything. The ultimate scoreboard, because only net margin pays the owner. All the elegance upstream is decoration if nothing survives to the bottom line.

Read the three as a set and you get a diagnosis: high gross with low operating margin means a great product inside a bloated machine, which can be an opportunity, if the operators tighten. Low gross margin means the product economics themselves are hard, and no operator can fully rescue them.

Margin Expansion: The Silent Return Driver

Now the dynamic part, and the reason this chapter matters more than almost any ratio you will ever compute.

A company growing revenue 25% with stable margins grows profits 25%. A company growing revenue 25% while its net margin climbs from 10 to 20 percent grows profits far faster than either number suggests. Growth multiplied by expansion, the compounding double engine behind almost every legendary stock of the modern era. And its mirror image is the great trap: fast revenue growth with thin margins and no credible path to thicker ones, growth that fills the top of the waterfall while nothing reaches the bottom, ever.

> *This leads to a conclusion that sounds contrarian and is merely arithmetic: growth without margins is fragile, while margins without growth can still compound. A business growing moderately with strong, defended margins and options is very often the better investment than a rocket with nothing left at the bottom line. Ideally you want both. Both is rare.*

When both is coming but has not arrived, the market routinely fails to see it, and that failure is one of the great sources of individual-investor returns. Palantir in 2022 was exactly this: still barely profitable on paper, dismissed accordingly, while gross margins in the eighties and visible operating leverage said that scale would mechanically convert into enormous net margins. That margin trajectory was most of my thesis. The market graded the company on the margin it had. The work graded it on the margin its structure implied. Structure won.

The forward question, always: not "what is the margin?" but "what does this margin profile look like in three years, and what has to be true for that?" You will never be precisely right. You only need to be roughly right. Margins are structural, so they move for reasons, and reasons can be studied.

Reading Margins Like a Structural Engineer

Trajectory over level, within an industry. Comparing a retailer's margins to a software company's is comparing a bridge to a bell tower. Compare against the company's own history and its direct competitors, and weight the direction most: expansion, quarter over quarter, is pricing power and scale compounding; erosion is competition inside the walls, visible here years before the revenue line admits it. The moat X-ray of Chapter 10 is, in daily practice, mostly a margin chart.

Asset-light versus asset-heavy.

Businesses that scale on code and brand can expand margins almost without limit as revenue grows; businesses that scale on factories and fleets must buy every increment of growth with capital. Neither is disqualifying; Tesla is asset-intensive and magnificent. But the ceiling and the reinvestment mathematics of Chapter 20 differ completely, and your projections in Chapter 19 must respect which physics apply.

But the deeper question is never light or heavy. It is the return the business earns on capital it must deploy.

Asset-heavy is only a curse when that capital compounds at low rates.

An asset-heavy business reinvesting at high returns, with room to keep doing it for years, is close to the best thing markets offer: a compounding machine that grows itself from the inside.

Amazon is the proven case, two decades of plowing every would-be dollar of profit back into fulfillment and cloud, until an "expensive" stock became one of the great compounders of the age.

Tesla is the same bet, still running.

The asset-light business often has the opposite problem: it gushes cash it cannot reinvest, and hands it back through buybacks. The ceiling and the reinvestment mathematics of Chapter 20 differ completely, and your projections in Chapter 19 must respect which physics apply.

Pricing power held in reserve.

The subtlest read of all, from Chapter 10's Costco discussion: some companies possess margin they deliberately decline to harvest, passing savings to customers to compound trust and volume instead. Reported margins understate these businesses permanently. The question is never just "what margin does it earn?" but "what margin could it earn if it chose?" – the gap between the two is stored energy, and it belongs to patient owners.

Revenue tells you how big a business is getting. Margins tell you how much of it ever reaches the owner. The market watches the first; your edge is in reading the second.

Part III, Chapter 17

Reading a 10-K Without Losing a Weekend

"If you read the annual report, you've done more than most people on Wall Street."

- Jim Rogers

Reading a 10-K Without Losing a Weekend

Somewhere in Stage Two of the funnel, a company earns the deepest document in public markets: the 10-K, the annual report filed with the SEC. Length varies, 50 pages for a simple business, 200 or more for a bank, but for the kind of serious, complex company you'll actually research, expect a 100 pages and up of everything it is legally required to tell you.

Most investors never open one. The minority who try often make the opposite mistake: they attempt to read it like a novel, drown by page 40, and never return. Both mistakes come from missing the same fact, the 10-K is not a book. It is a filing, assembled by lawyers to satisfy requirements, and large portions of it are boilerplate that repeats across every company in America. Inside those 100+ pages sit perhaps 20 to 30 pages of genuine signal. Your job is to extract them in one to two focused hours.

> *That is the 80/20 rule applied to the densest document you will ever use, and we are pragmatic here by design. You have work, a family, a life. Beating the market does not require infinite hours; it requires the right hours, placed correctly. A couple of hours per serious candidate, at the right stage, is plenty.*

When, Not Just How

Placement first, because the most common 10-K mistake is chronological.

The 10-K belongs in the second half of research, after the qualitative pass, after the statements have confirmed the story, when a company is a genuine finalist heading toward a real position. Reading a 100-page filing on a company you heard about on Tuesday is the single worst return on attention in investing: most candidates die in Stage One for reasons visible in an afternoon, and every hour of 10-K reading spent on a future corpse is an hour stolen from your finalists. The depth of research matches the weight of the intended position.

The 10-K is heavy machinery. Bring it in late.

The Efficient Pass

Work section by section, with a highlighter, in priority order.

Keep the annotated file, it becomes a running document you update annually, and by year three, your accumulated marginalia on a holding is worth more than most analyst reports.

- **Item 1 – Business.** The company describing itself: its segments, products, customers, and competition, and the best single narrative of how the machine works. Read it fully on first acquaintance. Highlight anything about customer concentration, because a business earning a third of its revenue from two customers is a different risk from what its income statement suggests, and note how the company characterizes its competition.
- **Item 1A – Risk Factors.** Trained skimming required. The first many pages are legal wallpaper: every company on earth faces "macroeconomic conditions" and "cybersecurity threats." You are hunting the specific risks, the named competitor, the patent cliff, the regulatory exposure unique to this business, the supplier that cannot be replaced. One reliable trick is to compare against last year's

filing. What got added is what the lawyers just became worried about, and the newest sentences in the oldest section are among the most informative in the document.

- **Item 7 – Management's Discussion and Analysis.** The heart of the filing, and worth half your total time. Management explains, in prose with numbers, why the results moved: what drove revenue, what happened to margins and costs, what they see ahead. This is where the waterfall of Chapter 14 gets its narration, and where management walks the segments, the businesses inside the business, because a great segment can hide inside a mediocre consolidated number for years. Read every word. Then hunt two things in the prose. First, the reconciliation between GAAP results and any "adjusted" figure management prefers, because what they add back, stock compensation, "one-time" charges that somehow recur every year, is a confession of how they want to be seen. Second, the metrics they choose to feature, watching especially for the key number that quietly disappears the year it stops flattering them.

- **Item 8 – Statements and, above all, the footnotes.** You have read the statements themselves in earlier stages. Here, the footnotes are the prize, and a handful earn most of your attention. Revenue recognition tells you how aggressively the company books its sales, and for a subscription business the same note holds deferred revenue and remaining performance obligations, the contracted revenue not yet recognized, one of the few honest leading indicators in the entire filing. The debt footnote schedules every maturity, so you can see which years the company is forced to refinance, and at what cost. Stock-based compensation is quantified here in full: the dilution that "adjusted" earnings politely leave out. The segment footnote carries the hard numbers behind the MD&A story, revenue and often operating profit for each business, so you can check the narration against the arithmetic. And the one almost nobody reads, related-party transactions, is where a company discloses the deals it does with its own insiders and affiliates. Skim with intent: revenue recognition, debt schedule, share-count mechanics, segments, anything labeled "commitments," anything involving an insider, anything that surprises you.

The auditor's tell.

One page you were never taught to read sits at the front of Item 8: the auditor's report. Since 2019, auditors of large companies must list their Critical Audit Matters, the accounts that required the most difficult, subjective judgment to sign off on. This is an independent party telling you exactly where the numbers are softest: a revenue-timing question, a goodwill estimate, a contingent liability. A company will never volunteer its riskiest estimates. Auditor are required to. Read those, then find the footnote each one points to.

The skippable mass.

Properties, standard legal proceedings (scan for anything existential, move on), market-for-securities boilerplate, controls attestations. Gone. This is where the other hundred pages were hiding.

What You Are Hunting

Across every section, the efficient reader carries the same three questions, and highlights only what answers them.

Does anything here contradict my thesis? You arrive at the 10-K already believing (that is why the company is a finalist) which makes this document your designated devil's advocate. A customer-concentration footnote, a risk factor naming a technology shift, a segment shrinking inside a growing total: the 10-K is where the funnel gets its last, best chance to kill the idea before capital arrives. Let it try.

Is anything material here that the market narrative ignores? The popular story about every company is built from headlines and calls; the 10-K contains the details the story omits: sometimes negative, sometimes gloriously positive, like a small segment compounding at rates that will dominate the company in five years.

And the annual delta: from the second year onward, you never re-read the whole filing; you read what changed. New risk factors, altered language around competition, segment re-definitions, footnotes that grew. A 10-K read against last year's takes forty minutes and yields more than the first read did.

One to two hours, twenty pages of signal, a highlighter, and the discipline to save it for last. That is the entire method, and it places you in the strange minority who have read the primary document of what they own.

The 10-K is the one place a company must tell you the truth in writing, once a year, under penalty of law.

It would be a shame to lose that to the hundred pages of wallpaper wrapped around it.

Part III, Chapter 18

Valuation I: What Is a Fair Price?

"The multiple is just the exchange rate between price and value."

Valuation I: What Is a Fair Price?

You have found a great business. Moats, operators, location, statements, everything holds. And none of it yet answers the question your money is about to ask: at what price?

Because here is the law of Part III: a stretched valuation turns a good business into a bad investment.

> *The company can be magnificent and the stock still ruinous, if the price you pay already contains the next decade of success plus a premium.*

People who bought the greatest companies of past eras at mania prices waited ten years to break even, on theses that were completely correct.

Being right about the business is half the job. This chapter is the other half.

There Is No Universal Formula

The first thing to unlearn is the idea that valuation is one calculation. Different kinds of businesses must be valued differently, and applying the wrong lens to the right company has cost investors more money than most crashes.

A value stock (mature, slow-growing, cash-rich) is valued on what it earns and returns today: earnings multiples, free cash flow yield, assets.

A dividend payer is valued on the durability and growth of its payout.

A growth company is valued on where its earnings are going, not where they are, which makes today's ratio almost meaningless on its own and shifts the work to forecasting the trajectory, roughly right rather than precisely wrong.

A cyclical is the trap category: it looks cheapest at the peak of its cycle (fat earnings, low P/E, about to reverse) and most expensive at the trough, the one type where the naive ratio actively lies to you.

The classic casualty of lens confusion was Amazon, which "looked absurdly expensive" on P/E for a decade while it deliberately converted every dollar of would-be profit into reinvestment. Investors using the value-stock lens missed one of the great compounders of the age because they brought the wrong ruler. Chapter 16 told you which physics a business runs on. Valuation begins by choosing the ruler that matches.

The P/E, Understood In Context

For profitable growth companies, the core of this book's universe, the working ruler is the price-to-earnings multiple: what you pay per dollar of annual earnings. A P/E of 25 means 25 dollars per dollar of current earnings. Two upgrades make it usable.

First, look forward, not just backward. Trailing P/E uses the past year; forward P/E uses expected earnings. For a company growing fast, the difference is enormous. The expensive-looking trailing number can hide a reasonable forward one, and you are buying the future, not the receipts. You can push it a step further still and ask what the two-year or three-year forward P/E implies once the earnings you expect have arrived.

Second, and this is the entire key: a P/E is never high or low in isolation. It is high or low relative to growth.

In recent decades the market as a whole has mostly traded between 18 and 26 times trailing earnings; that band is the fair price for an average company growing at an average rate. Which immediately reframes every number you will ever see: a P/E of 30 is expensive for a company growing 8% and a gift for one compounding earnings at 30%. The ratio means nothing until it is placed next to the growth rate.

The Lynch Rule

Peter Lynch compressed this relationship into the most useful single sentence in valuation: the P/E of a fairly priced company will roughly equal its long-term earnings growth rate.

Growing EPS at 20% a year? A multiple around 20 is fair. Growing at 35? A multiple around 35 is defensible. From this one rule, a mental map draws itself, a matrix with the multiple on one axis and growth on the other.

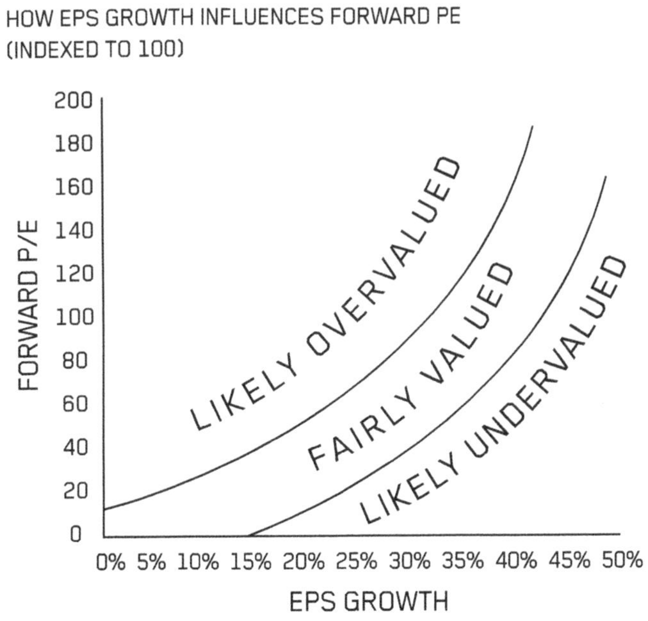

Along the diagonal, fair value. Below it, a company growing 25% trading at 15 times: the undervalued zone where fortunes start. Far above it, 15% growth at an 80 multiple: the too-hot zone, where years of future success are pre-paid to someone else.

And one region is simply mythical: quality compounders growing 50% at a P/E of 12 do not exist outside crashes, which is one more reason Chapter 8 keeps the chest full.

The rule is a compass, not a court ruling. But it converts every stock quote from a mystery into a question with a method: what growth does this price assume, and is that assumption believable?

A Worked Example

Here is the compass on a real position, with round numbers from my own AMD work.

The company earns $3.40 per share, trailing. The research from Part III's earlier chapters (data-center demand, margin trajectory toward roughly 25% net) supports a path to about $11 of EPS within three to four years. Getting from $3.40 to $11 requires compounding earnings around 35% annually.

By the Lynch rule, a forward multiple in the mid-thirties is therefore defensible, so with the stock trading at points where the forward multiple sat far below that, the matrix placed it in the undervalued zone even as headlines called the whole sector expensive on trailing numbers.

Notice what did the work: the earnings path, which came from the funnel, the margin chapter, the statements. Valuation is always the last step of research, never a substitute for it. The multiple only tells you what the market assumes. Whether the assumption is wrong is something only the work can know.

Three warnings seal the chapter. Never buy a low P/E by itself. Cheapness has causes, and the market prices dying businesses like dying businesses; a low multiple on collapsing earnings is a trap, not a bargain. Never pay any price for quality, that is how the too-hot zone recruits its victims, and even Palantir was only a great investment because 2020-2023 offered it at prices that assumed failure. And hold your estimates loosely: the growth rate in your matrix is a forecast, and Chapter 19 is about building forecasts honest enough to bet on.

Price is what you pay; value is what you get. Buffett's oldest line, and the entire chapter in nine words.

The multiple is just the exchange rate between the two. Learn to read it, and the market starts showing you its assumptions.

Part III, Chapter 19

Valuation II: Projections

"It is better to be roughly right than precisely wrong."

- John Maynard Keynes

Valuation II: Projections

Chapter 18 gave you the compass. This chapter teaches you to draw the map, the projection: a disciplined, numerical estimate of what a company will earn over the next three to five years, and therefore what its shares can reasonably be worth.

Two announcements before the spreadsheet opens. First, this is the final stage of the funnel, performed only on finalists, for the reasons Chapter 13 established. A projection built on a business you have not qualitatively verified is precision applied to fiction.

Second, and this is the emotional key to the whole chapter: the goal is to be roughly right, never precisely wrong. You do not need fifteen decimal points. Business is messy; investing is messy. A projection is not a prophecy, it is a structured way of asking what has to be true for this price to make sense, answered with numbers.

The Machine, Step by Step

Every projection is the income statement of Chapter 14 run forward. Five steps.

- **Step 1 – Revenue.** There are two ways to build the revenue line, and choosing the right one is half the craft of this step. The first is top-down, for businesses whose revenue is a broad stream with no countable parts. Start from the demonstrated growth rate, then adjust for what you know: the supertrend runway of Chapter 12, guidance graded by the Chapter 11 promise ledger, and the law of large numbers – growth decelerates with scale, and a projection holding 40% growth flat for five years is fiction. Though not a law of physics: for some companies, flawless execution bends the curve the other way for years. Recognizing which is the soft art, trained only by repetition. The second is bottom-up, and where it applies, it is strictly better: units sold times average selling price. If you can count the units, count them. My first serious model was Tesla, 2018, when the argument was whether the company could produce cars at all. I did not model a growth percentage; I modeled deliveries times price per vehicle, and while the bears argued sentiment, my spreadsheet counted units. Subscribers times monthly price, patients times revenue per patient: whenever the business sells countable things, build from the units up. A bottom-up model is testable every quarter at the part level, which the top-down method can never give you. Either way, the step ends the same: a revenue line for each of the next three to five years.

- **Step 2 – Margin.** The Chapter 16 work becomes the engine here: what net margin is reasonable at each future revenue level? Anchor in the demonstrated trajectory, the physics of the model (asset-light or heavy), and comparable companies at the scale your target is heading toward. This assumption moves the answer more than any other, treat it with care.

- **Step 3 – Net income.** Revenue times margin, per year. The arithmetic is trivial; every gram of difficulty lived in the two assumptions above.

- **Step 4 – EPS.** Divide by the share count, the future share count, honoring the dilution or buyback pattern the company has shown (Chapter

15). A company diluting 3% annually has a visibly different EPS future than one retiring shares, at identical net income.

- **Step 5 – Price.** Apply a defensible future multiple to the final-year EPS, the Lynch logic of Chapter 18, applied to the growth rate the company will have then, not now. A company growing 35% today but 20% in year four should be valued in year four like a 20% grower. Assigning today's excitement to tomorrow's maturity is the most common way honest projections are corrupted.

Here is the machine on AMD, the example from Chapter 18 with its gears exposed: trailing EPS of $3.40; analyst consensus and my own demand work pointing to over $10 the following year; revenue growth held at a decelerating schedule thereafter; net margin ramped to 25% and held. Not heroic for a company of that quality at scale; the resulting path landing near $30 of EPS in three to four years; a mid-twenties to thirties multiple on that maturity implying a price range far above the quote at the time of the work.

Five steps, one page, and suddenly the daily price is not information anymore, it is an offer the market is giving you.

Before trusting any model, triangulate it against the two other estimates that always exist: analyst consensus and management guidance.

It is calibration. If your numbers land near consensus, you have likely modeled correctly and learned that the price already contains your view. If they diverge, one of two things is true: you have made an error, or you have found an edge. Both are valuable, and the work is finding out which.

Check your assumptions first, a wrong share count or an impossible margin ramp is usually the answer. But when the assumptions survive inspection and the divergence remains, you are holding the only thing that ever beats the market: a defensible view the market does not share. My Palantir model diverged from consensus for two years. The consensus moved.

Three Futures, Not One

A single projection is a guess. The professional version runs the machine three times.

> *The base case uses your honest central assumptions, what you expect. The bull case asks: if the thesis works better than expected, with margins overshooting and the runway extending, where does it land? The bear case is the one that earns its keep: growth disappoints, margins stall, the multiple compresses to market-average. Build it with genuine pessimism.*

The three cases give you a range, and the range is the decision. If today's price sits near or below the bear case, the market is paying you to take a risk it has overestimated.

That is the asymmetry behind every great entry in this book, from Palantir under ten dollars to the 2020 deployments. If the price already needs the bull case, everything has to go right just to break even. And everything never goes right. You are hunting the opposite: a price where being roughly right pays enormously, and being wrong costs little.

Maintenance

A projection is a living document with a quarterly appointment.

Each earnings report, hold reality against the map: revenue

on path or off, margins arriving on schedule or stalling? Small wobbles are weather. A genuine divergence means the model updates in whichever direction the evidence points, including the painful one.

And this discipline solves the problem that torments every holder of a winner: the stock that ran 80% in a year. The question is never "am I up too much?" it is "what does the updated projection say from today?" Sometimes the business grew faster than the stock and the map shows more room than before. Sometimes the price sprinted past every case you can defend, and the map is telling you something Chapter 23 will teach you to act on.

The projection, updated, is also the only honest defense against both euphoria and panic, 2022 did not frighten me out of Palantir because the map, rebuilt each quarter from actual results, kept disagreeing with the price. When you own a map, the crowd's screaming becomes data about the crowd.

You will be wrong constantly. Every projection I have ever built missed the specifics. It does not matter. The discipline of building them is what forces you to understand the machine well enough to hold it; the range is what tells you when the price is an insult or a gift.

The statisticians settled this long ago: all models are wrong, but some are useful, and a projection is exactly that kind of model.

> *Precisely wrong is what the analysts sell. Roughly right is what compounds.*

Draw the map. Then let the market wander, it always comes home to the territory.

Part III, Chapter 20

Capital Allocation: What They Do With the Money

"After ten years on the job, a CEO whose company annually retains earnings equal to 10% of net worth will have been responsible for the deployment of more than 60% of all the capital at work in the business."

- Warren Buffett

Capital Allocation: What They Do With the Money

Two companies. Similar revenue, earnings, growth. A decade later, one has compounded its shareholders' capital many times over. The other, despite equally healthy profits every single year, has gone nowhere.

You have met this puzzle twice already, Chapter 10 solved one version with moats, Chapter 16 another with margins. Here is the third and final mechanism, the one that operates after the profits are safely earned: what management does with the cash.

Many companies generate profits. Very few compound them well. The difference is called capital allocation, and it is simultaneously one of the most important and least understood forces in investing.

> *The stakes are simple to state. When a business earns a dollar, that dollar gets used exactly once. A management team that repeatedly deploys dollars at high returns is running a compounding machine inside the compounding machine you already own. A team that deploys them badly is a leak in the hull. Draining, year after year, the very profits that made the company look attractive.*

The Six Doors

Every dollar of free cash flow exits through one of six doors. Learn the doors, and every capital-allocation decision becomes gradable.

- **Reinvest in the business.** R&D, capacity, new markets. Usually the best door, when the returns are there, because money compounding inside a moat at high rates is exactly what you bought the company for. The grading test is the return on that reinvested capital: a business earning 25% on each plowed-back dollar should plow back everything it can; a business earning 6% on reinvestment is burning your money to buy the CEO a bigger empire. This is why Amazon suppressing profits for a decade was brilliant and a declining retailer "investing in transformation" is tragic.

- **Acquire other companies.** The most dangerous door, because it is the most fun for executives. Acquisitions are graded on price paid versus value received, and the empirical record of large corporate acquisitions is grim. Deals done at auction prices, in hot markets, justified by "synergies" that footnotes later bury as goodwill impairments (Chapter 15's serial-acquirer flag). Small, disciplined, repeated tuck-ins by proven operators are the honorable exception.

- **Buy back shares.** Genuinely brilliant or genuinely destructive, with not much in between, and the difference is price. Retiring shares below intrinsic value permanently concentrates every future dollar of earnings into your remaining shares, the quiet engine of some of the greatest compounding records ever. Buying back stock at peak prices, with debt, to flatter the EPS on which bonuses vest, is the same mechanism run in reverse. Chapter 18's toolkit tells you which one you are watching: was the stock cheap when they bought it?

- **Pay dividends.** The honest door, cash returned, undeniable, the ultimate proof of Tenet 16 that the cash was ever real. Its cost is the tax drag and a confession: a growing dividend says management sees fewer high-return reinvestment options than before. Correct for a mature fortress; a yellow flag on a company still claiming a vast growth runway.

- **Pay down debt.** Unglamorous, occasionally optimal. Transforming the balance sheet from vulnerable to fortress ahead of the storms Chapter 8 promises are coming.
- **Sit on the cash.** Despised by analysts, and yet, you of all readers know better. A company holding cash while prices are silly, then deploying aggressively into dislocation, is running the war chest doctrine at corporate scale. Berkshire Hathaway's decades of "lazy" billions, deployed violently into every crisis, is Chapter 8 with a stock ticker.

Six doors. None automatically right. The grade is always the same question: at what rate of return did this dollar exit?

Reading the Allocator

You never grade a speech; you grade a record, and the record is public.

Pull five to ten years of history and trace the dollars. What has this team done with the cash flow, and what happened next? Acquisitions from five years ago: growing, or impaired? Buybacks: clustered at low prices or at euphoric tops? Share count: shrinking, or inflating through stock compensation while "buybacks" merely mop up the dilution, the treadmill that returns nothing to owners while consuming billions? Return on invested capital across the period: is each retained dollar still earning its keep, or has scale pushed marginal returns below what you could earn yourself?

Then cross-examine against Chapter 11's incentives, because allocation follows compensation with embarrassing reliability: executives paid on EPS buy back stock at any price; executives paid on revenue acquire anything that moves; executives who own the company allocate like owners. The proxy statement predicts the capital allocation record before it happens.

And here the founder thread from Chapter 11 completes itself. The reason founder-led companies recur in this book, and in my portfolio, is capital allocation horizon: an owner-operator deploying cash asks "what maximizes this business in 2035?", while a five-year CEO asks what maximizes the optics before their options vest.

Both are rational. Only one is compounding on your schedule.

The Owner's Posture

A last reframe, which is really the posture of this entire book.

As a shareholder you have outsourced the CEO's job, but not the owner's.

You sit, in a real sense, above the CEO: your capital, their stewardship. And your two owner's powers are exactly the ones this chapter trains: judge the allocation record accurately, and act on the judgment. Agree with how they deploy your profits, as I do with the teams running my seven, and entrust them with more.

Watch a team squander three years of cash flow on vanity acquisitions and buyback-at-the-top games, and exercise the sacred right the private business owner envies: take your capital and leave, in one afternoon, at the click of a button.

A company is ultimately a machine for turning today's profits into tomorrow's value, and management's capital allocation is the gearbox of that machine.

Buy great gearboxes. The engine's horsepower is wasted on anything less.

Part III, Chapter 21

Macro: What to Ignore and What to Understand

"You can't predict. You can prepare."

- Howard Marks

Macro: What to Ignore and What to Understand

Turn on any financial channel, any hour of any day, and you will find brilliant-sounding people discussing the same rotating cast of questions. Where are interest rates going? Is a recession coming? What will the election mean for markets? What about China, oil, the dollar, the deficit?

This chapter's thesis can be stated in one sentence, and I will spend the rest of the pages defending it: for the long-term investor, macro forecasting is a waste of time, and behaving as if it were not is one of the most expensive habits in markets.

The Complexity Wall

List what "macro" contains.

- **Monetary policy** – rates, tightening, easing, the reaction functions of central banks.
- **Fiscal policy** – deficits, taxation, stimulus. Inflation dynamics – supply chains, wages, energy, commodities.
- **Growth and the business cycle** – GDP, employment, consumer spending, recessions.
- **Inflation dynamics** – supply chains, wages, energy, commodities.
- **Credit and liquidity** – bank lending, credit spreads, the plumbing of the financial system.
- **Geopolitics** – wars, sanctions, trade restrictions, regime changes.
- **Currencies.**
- **Sovereign debt.**

- **Black swans by definition unlistable** – pandemics, financial crises.

And floating above all of it, the market psychology through which every one of these forces is filtered before it touches a price.

Now notice the structure of that list: every item is a system of extreme complexity, low predictability, and zero controllability, and every item depends on the others.

Interest rates depend on inflation, which depends on energy and wages, which depend on geopolitics and job markets, which depend on things nobody saw coming.

You could command a hundred PhD-level analysts and still fail, because one pandemic, one war, one bank failure throws every model out of sync at once, and reliably does, every few years.

> *This is not a claim that macro does not matter. It matters enormously. It is a claim about predictability: the people who forecast these systems for a living are, measured honestly, roughly coin-flippers. And unlike you, they are at least paid for flipping. Nobody gets it right every time. Nobody gets it right reliably at all. The strange cultural fact is that we all know this, and the forecasting industry thrives anyway, because macro talk feels sophisticated and micro work feels like homework.*

Here is the reframe that changes behavior: attention is capital. Every hour spent handicapping the next Fed meeting is an hour not spent reading a 10-K, and only one of those hours compounds.

Macro versus micro is a decision about where your edge lives. Macro is complex, unpredictable, uncontrollable. Micro (specific companies, their moats and margins) is knowable, analyzable, yours. Choose.

	Macro	Micro
Complexity	High	Bounded
Predictability	Low	Analyzable
Control	None	Choose what to own

Amateurs want predictions. Professionals want systems. If your success depends on guessing the next rate move, the next headline, the next quarter's GDP, you are playing a fool's game against opponents who own the casino.

What You Keep

Rejecting forecasting is not rejecting understanding. A short list of macro literacy serves the stock picker, as context, never as trigger.

Rates are gravity. Interest rates set the price of the future: when they rise, tomorrow's earnings are worth less today, and the multiples of Chapter 18 compress, hardest for companies whose value sits furthest in the future.

You hold this knowledge not to predict rates but to interpret without panic: 2022 was substantially this force acting on multiples, which is exactly why falling prices on strengthening businesses read as sway, not collapse. The gravity explains the weather. It says nothing about which buildings stand.

Cycles exist; timing them does not. Expansion, euphoria, contraction, despair, recovery. The wheel has turned this way for a century and will keep turning. You cannot know the dates. You do not need to: the war chest doctrine is cycle-awareness without cycle-prediction. Permanently prepared, never forecasting, deploying on the panic you were promised rather than the schedule you guessed.

> *Position zour portfolio to survive whatever comes. Nobody gets the macro right every time, the design goal is a portfolio that does not require getting it right: fortress balance sheets that refinance nothing in a credit winter, businesses that grip harder in recessions, a reserve that converts crisis into shopping. Survival is a portfolio property, not a prediction skill. Zou build it in, once, and then the forecasts stop mattering.*

Macro as tailwind check, at the company level only. The one legitimate analytical use: when studying a specific business, ask which large forces touch it specifically. Rate sensitivity for a lender like SoFi, government budget cycles for Palantir, consumer strength for the retailers whose earnings I skim precisely as an economic thermometer. Note the direction of causation: you study the company and consult the macro, never the reverse. "Rates will fall so buy growth stocks" is forecasting in a trench coat.

The Payoff of Ignoring Well

Run the counterfactual on my own record. An investor who correctly weighted the macro consensus would have been out of the market in 2020 (pandemic, obviously), out again in 2022 (inflation, war, recession certain), and cautious through 2023's disbelief rally. Impeccably informed, thrice wrong, and poorer at every step than the investor who ignored all of it and kept verifying that his seven companies were executing. The years the consensus was most confidently bearish were precisely the years my heaviest capital went in. That is not because I forecasted better. It is because I was not forecasting at all.

> *The market rewards those who study what can be known and hold through what cannot.*

So delete the forecast habit entirely, and replace it with the only macro position this book endorses: prepared for everything, predicting nothing.

Let the brilliant people argue about the weather. You own the buildings.

Part III, Chapter 22

Special Situations

"Companies go public when it is most favorable for them, not for you."

Special Situations: The IPO Cycle and Other Traps

Most of Part III applies to any company at any time. This chapter covers the situations with their own physics: the newly public company, the turnaround, the cyclical. In each, the standard tools work only after you understand the special rules. One of these situations has produced more of my portfolio's value than any other single pattern, so we start there.

The First Rule of IPOs

Begin with the incentive structure, because it explains everything that follows: companies go public when it is most favorable for them, not for you.

> *An IPO is a sale, and the sellers choose the timing. They come to market when excitement is high, when the sector is hot, when insiders who built the company for a decade can finally cash out at a full price. Nobody rings the bell at the bottom of the market or in the depths of sector pessimism. Which means the IPO price is, structurally, close to the most optimistic price the company can command, set by bankers whose explicit job is maximizing it. Buying at the IPO is buying at the moment of maximum marketing from the best-informed sellers on earth.*

And yet, hold both thoughts: some of the greatest investments of this era were recent IPOs. Including my largest position. The resolution of the paradox is timing within a cycle that repeats with startling regularity.

The Cycle

Watch what happened to the 2020–2021 IPO cohort, because the same movie played four times in my own coverage.

- **Phase one:** the hype bump. The debut, the coverage, the scarcity of shares, the enthusiasm. Price detaches from fundamentals and runs. Palantir listed near $10 and rode the mania toward $39 within months. SoFi, Hims & Hers, same arc.
- **Phase two:** the consolidation desert. The excitement exhausts itself, lockups expire, insiders sell, the market moves to the next shiny debut, and the stock falls hard, then goes nowhere for two or three years. Palantir spent 2022 at six to eight dollars, declared dead. Hims drifted sideways for years as a forgotten SPAC. SoFi sat range-bound while the narrative called it just another fintech. This desert is where the crowd's conclusion becomes "the IPO failed", and where the actual opportunity assembles, because through all of it, the businesses were executing: revenue compounding, losses narrowing, moats deepening, unwatched.
- **Phase three:** fundamentals catch up. Over time, the numbers become undeniable. Profitability arrives, the growth persists another year, then another, and the price re-rates violently to meet the business it had ignored. Everyone who bought the desert looks like a genius. Everyone who bought the hype is, often years later, still underwater on companies that succeeded.

The long-term investor's playbook writes itself from the anatomy. Ignore the debut completely, let the traders have the bump. Add the interesting ones to the Chapter 13 watch list. Then research through the desert, when nobody cares, when the funnel can work without a crowd, and build the position in the consolidation, sized by the evidence, exactly as the Chapter 9 doctrine prescribes. Hims in the single digits with profitability arriving was this playbook executed in full; the buyer there was up fourfold within a couple of years, not by predicting anything, but by buying a working business during the years the market was bored of it. Palantir at seven was the same trade at jugular scale.

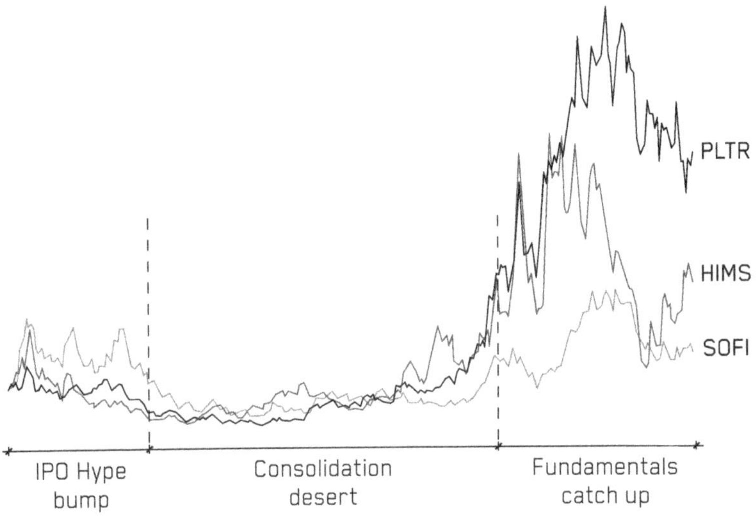

One caution completes the pattern: the desert also holds companies that die there. The smaller and younger the company, the more proof of performance you demand before capital moves. The phase-two buy signal is never the low price. It is the fundamentals inflecting while the price still sleeps.

Turnarounds: The Siren Song

The second special situation is the famous fallen company at a nostalgic price, and the rule is brutal because the base rate is brutal: most turnarounds do not turn.

The seduction is powerful, a brand you grew up with, a stock down 80%, a new CEO with a plan. But a great business in temporary trouble (2022's entire market) and a deteriorating business in permanent decline are different species wearing the same chart, and the difference is the moat autopsy: temporary trouble leaves the moat intact: customers still captive, pricing power dormant, the problem cyclical or self-inflicted and fixable. Decline means the moat is breached, with customers structurally leaving and the industry moving away. No CEO oratory rebuilds it. The graveyard is full of inventions made obsolete, and full of investors who bought them cheap all the way down. If you must fish here, demand a strong surviving core and wait for actual signs of revival in the numbers, never buy the plan. Buy the evidence, or nothing.

Cyclicals: The Ratio That Lies

Chapter 18 flagged it; here is the mechanism. In cyclical industries (semiconductors, energy, autos, shipping) earnings swell and collapse with the cycle, so the P/E inverts its meaning: at the cycle peak, earnings are maximal and the ratio looks cheap, precisely when the only direction is down; at the trough, earnings have vanished and the ratio looks infinite, precisely when recovery is nearest. The naive value signal fires backwards at both ends. Cyclicals are ownable; AMD carries cyclical exposure inside its secular story. But they are valued on normalized, through-cycle earnings and position in the cycle, never on the trailing ratio. If you cannot locate where in the cycle you are standing, you are guessing.

Three situations, one shared grammar: in each, the market's default reading of the surface (the exciting debut, the cheap legend, the low ratio) is systematically wrong, and the correction comes from the same deep tools this Part already gave you, applied with the special rules in mind.

Special situations are where patience gets paid its largest premiums, because the crowd's clock runs on excitement, and yours runs on evidence.

Part III, Chapter 23

Selling: The Hardest Chapter

"Selling your winners and holding your losers is like cutting the flowers and watering the weeds."

- Peter Lynch

Selling: The Hardest Chapter

An entire book about buying and holding eventually owes you the other half of the transaction. And I have saved it for the end of Part III deliberately, because every good selling decision is built from the tools that came before it.

Let me open with the question I am asked more than any other, in exactly the form it arrives: "I am up 200% on a stock. Should I take profits?"

The answer is that the question, as asked, contains a hidden error, and removing the error resolves not just this decision but every selling decision you will ever face.

Your Gain Is Irrelevant

> *Here is the error: the 200% is information about the past, and the market does not price the past. Whether you are up 200%, down 40%, or exactly flat, the shares are worth the same tonight, and tomorrow's return will be identical for every holder regardless of their entry. Your cost basis is an emotional fact, not a financial one.*

So the only question that ever matters is asked from today, facing forward: given everything I now know, does this company offer the returns I require from here? And the tool that answers it already exists, the Chapter 19 projection, updated with the quarters that have passed. Rerun the machine from today's numbers. Two outcomes are possible.

The projection still shows a credible path to your required return, the business grew along with, or faster than, the price, and today's quote still sits at or below your base case. Then you hold, regardless of the size of the gain, and the tax code applauds: not selling means not paying capital gains, not searching for a replacement idea, not interrupting Chapter 5's compounding.

> *This is the ideal career: buy so well, and reverify so honestly, that you are never forced out. The people who bought the generational compounders a decade ago and simply held are the wealthiest cohort this market ever produced.*

Or the honest rerun shows the price has consumed the future. Even the reasonable path from today offers pedestrian returns, and the bull case is needed just to match the market. Then, and only then, has a sale earned its justification, when the forward return no longer clears the bar, and better returns exist elsewhere in your funnel.

Beginners jump between positions at every 50% gain, perpetually harvesting seedlings to buy new seeds. The competent sell for one reason only: the map, redrawn from today, no longer supports the position.

Solid Reasons and Fake Ones

Generalize that logic and the complete selling doctrine fits in two lists.

Sell for structure. The thesis is broken: the moat breached, the numbers confirming decline, the projection dead even in the bull case. Or management has disqualified itself by the standards of Chapters 11 and 20. Or the price has traveled so far beyond every defensible case that the forward return is gone.

Or, there is a rare and legitimate example, a dramatically superior opportunity requires the capital, and the gap is large enough to pay the taxes and the uncertainty of being wrong twice.

Never sell for weather. The price fell (that alone is a fact about moods, not businesses); headlines are frightening (they always are); a forecast says recession (Chapter 21 in its entirety); you are up a round number (this chapter's opening error); or you are bored (Chapter 27's disease, wearing a rationale).

Every fake reason has the same signature, it originates in the price or in your feelings about the price, never in the business. If the sentence justifying your sale does not contain a fact about the company, you are not selling. You are flinching.

The Stop-Loss Delusion

One selling mechanism deserves demolition by name, because brokers offer it as prudence: the stop-loss, the standing order that sells automatically when the price falls to a chosen level.

For a trader, coherent. For a long-term investor, a machine for converting sway into permanent loss. It is Chapter 4's exact failure mode, automated. I watched it play out on a single Monday in August 2024: an overnight unwind in Japanese markets gapped the Nasdaq down at the open, individual names fell 10, 15 percent in minutes, Palantir among them.

By the close the day had nearly fully recovered, as if nothing happened. Every stop-loss in that airgap executed at the bottom: position gone, sold to someone calmer, a taxable event crystallized on years of gains, and then the impossible psychology of buying back higher what you were just forced out of. Nothing about any business changed that day. Only prices did, briefly, and the automated sellers paid for the privilege of reacting.

The deeper tell is philosophical: a stop-loss is a written confession that you do not know what you own, that a falling price would be information rather than, as it is for the prepared, an invitation.

We welcome declines in companies we understand; a machine that flees them is the opposite of everything in this book. Your protection was never an order type. It was Chapter 4: knowing the difference between a falling price and a failing business.

Trimming and the Second Decision

Finally, the partial sale, and a return to Chapter 7's hardest teaching. Mechanical trimming of winners back to "sensible" weights is how flowers get cut to water weeds; my refusal to trim the position that grew to half my portfolio was not negligence but the projection, rerun quarterly, continuing to say yes. Trimming is legitimate exactly where full sales are: when the updated map says the forward return has genuinely thinned, or when a position's size has exceeded not your rules but your verified knowledge. Trim to the depth of your research, never to the comfort of a percentage.

Selling is not the opposite of holding. Both are the same act, obeying the updated map, with different answers.

You will hold when others panic and sell when others celebrate, for one reason: you reran the projection this morning and know what the stock can realistically return from here. Everyone else is just watching the price.

PART IV:
THE BUILDING RISES

Part IV, Chapter 24

When the Game Changes

"What got you here won't get you there."

- Marshall Goldsmith

When the Game Changes

Part IV begins at a threshold most investing books never reach, because most investing books are written for the climb. This part is written for the altitude.

Somewhere past the first million, without a ceremony, the game you have been playing ends and a different one begins. Same market and same tickers, entirely different physics. Most investors cross the threshold without noticing, keep playing by the old rules, and pay heavily for the lag. This chapter is the briefing I wish someone had handed me at the border.

The Death of the Contribution

The first change is arithmetic, and it is emotional dynamite.

For your entire climb, the monthly deposit was the hero. In the early years it was the growth, and every disciplined transfer visibly moved the number. Now run today's math: a $1,500 monthly contribution into a $1.5 million portfolio is a tenth of a percent. The portfolio's ordinary daily weather moves more than your month of discipline. The deposits that built the building can no longer sway it.

I can date my own noticing precisely. The ledger dates it for me. In 2024 I deposited €32,782 across the whole year.

Disciplined, respectable sum. That year, there were mornings when the portfolio moved more before breakfast. Ordinary Tuesdays with ordinary volatility. The first time I caught it, I sat with the screen for a while, feeling something I had no name for. Half a decade of identity was built on being the person who feeds the machine, yet the machine had quietly stopped noticing the meals.

This produces a strange grief nobody warns you about: the ritual that carried you for a decade suddenly means nothing measurable. The correct response is to understand what happened: your capital stopped being a stream and became a stock.

> *The portfolio is now the engine and the fuel at once. Returns on the existing base dwarf anything you can add to it, which means the levers of Chapter 3 have formally rotated for the last time: capital built the base, growth rate multiplied it, and from here, time and temperament do nearly all remaining work.*

Keep contributing (the habit protects the discipline) but know that your job description changed. You are no longer feeding a machine. You are steering one.

Positions Matter

The second change follows directly: at scale, only meaningful positions move the needle, and meaningful is now a large number.

A 50% gain on a $5,000 flyer was real money on a $60,000 portfolio. On $1.5 million it is noise, a third of a percent, invisible inside a normal week. This is the arithmetic behind Chapter 13's sharpest line: one great $300k position can move your portfolio; ten cute $5k trades cannot. And yet watch what most investors do at exactly this stage: they diversify into dozens of small "interesting" positions, precisely when small positions have lost all remaining purpose. The breadcrumb portfolio at seven figures is all of the effort of concentration with none of its power.

If that still feels reckless at seven figures, look up.

Bill Ackman's Pershing Square runs its concentrated strategy on more than twenty billion dollars, and it builds the whole thing on what the firm calls eight to twelve core holdings.

A manager with thousands of times your capital chooses to own about the same number of companies this book asks you to.

> *Concentration is not a phase you grow out of once the numbers get serious. It is the discipline that made the numbers serious in the first place, and the professionals who compound at scale hold it tighter, not looser.*

And notice which way scale actually cuts. A twenty-billion-dollar fund is pushed toward more names by its own size: it cannot take a meaningful stake in a great smaller company without swallowing the whole float or moving the price against itself. You have the opposite problem, which is to say no problem at all.

At two or five million you can own exactly the businesses you want, at exactly the weights your research justifies, with none of the constraints that force the giants to spread. If Ackman can stay that concentrated with all of that working against him, you have no excuse to scatter with all of it working for you.

So the doctrine tightens rather than loosens. The same seven to twelve companies, but the pillars now measured in hundreds of thousands, sized by the Chapter 9 framework with a new sobriety, because the other side of the arithmetic arrived too: a 30% drawdown on a $700k position is a different lived experience than the same percentage on a flyer, however identical the math claims to be.

> *Return was never just a number. It is a function of scale, duration, and above all, conviction.*

Every dollar has a job. Every risk needs a reason. Your

tolerance is no longer how you feel about volatility; it is a design decision tied to what each layer of the machine is for.

Meaningful position sizes also change how you buy. A $300,000 position cannot be opened the way a $5,000 one could, in one click on one afternoon.

It is built gradually: a starter tranche, evidence, another tranche, months of construction. Which means the research now has a new customer, asking one blunt question before every deployment: do you know this company well enough to give it a year of your salary?

At this scale, conviction is no longer a feeling you have. It is a load rating you certify.

The Interior Change

And the last change is not in the portfolio at all.

At this scale the portfolio stops being a project and becomes a presence. A second household member whose daily moods are measured in months of your salary. A red week now "costs" more than your car; an ordinary correction erases years of contributions on paper.

If your relationship to the number is what it was at $80,000, checking daily, feeling daily, the altitude will grind you down precisely because nothing has gone wrong.

The professionals at this level all converge on the same adaptation: they widen the reporting period. Judge quarters, not days. Let the daily number become what it always was, weather data about strangers' moods, and reserve your attention for the only questions that were ever yours: are the businesses executing, is the map current, is the structure sound.

The game changed because you won the first one. That was

the point. The climb built the capital. The altitude tests the character, and the next three chapters are about exactly that.

Part IV, Chapter 25

Stillness Is a Strategy

"The most profitable thing I did in three years was, measurably, nothing."

Stillness Is a Strategy

Here is a fact from my own records that took me years to appreciate: in the last three years, during which my portfolio grew by well over a million dollars, my total activity in my largest position was zero. Not one share bought. Not one share sold. Twelve thousand shares of Palantir, untouched, through a twelvefold rise, through headlines calling it overvalued at every step, through a thousand invitations to be clever.

> *The most profitable thing I did in those three years was, measurably, nothing, and this chapter is about why nothing is the hardest skill in this book, and the most valuable one at scale.*

The Tinkering Instinct

Every force in your environment is engineered against stillness.

Your broker profits from your activity and gamified the app accordingly. Financial media must generate urgency daily or die; every day is "pivotal," every event a "turning point."

Your own psychology is the worst conspirator of all: you spent years building competence, the competence is real, and competence begs to be used. Doing nothing feels like negligence. Adjusting, optimizing, rotating. That feels like work, like earning the returns.

But run the audit every honest investor runs. Take your last twenty discretionary actions: the trims, the rotations, the "taking some off the table," the tactical repositioning. Price the counterfactual of having done none of them. For almost everyone, the do-nothing portfolio wins, and not narrowly.

Fidelity's famous internal finding pointed the same direction: their best-performing accounts belonged disproportionately to investors who had forgotten they had accounts. The activity was never the work. The work was done years ago, in the funnel, in the research, in the buying. Activity after that point is mostly the slow vandalism of your own earlier judgment.

This is the tinkering instinct, and at seven figures it is your single largest liability, bigger than any macro risk, bigger than any position. Chapter 24 established the arithmetic: at scale, one unnecessary exit from a compounder costs more than a decade of clever adjustments can earn back. The tinkerer at $60,000 loses opportunities. The tinkerer at $1.5 million loses fortunes.

One condition underwrites this entire result, and it must be said or the chapter becomes dangerous: doing nothing only wins when the first part was done correctly.

Stillness is the reward for positioning, for buying great businesses at defensible prices after real research. Hold a portfolio of mistakes still for a decade and the market will simply deliver the losses undisturbed. The work happens upfront; the stillness is what the work purchased.

What Stillness Is Not

Now the crucial distinction, because stillness practiced wrong is just neglect.

Stillness is not ignorance. Every quarter, the full inspection runs exactly as Part III taught: earnings graded, projections rerun, promise ledgers updated, moats X-rayed through the margin lines. The stillness of this chapter is aggressively informed.

It is the decision, made from complete current knowledge,

that no action is warranted. Neglect is not looking; stillness is looking, verifying, and declining to move. From the outside the two are indistinguishable for years. In the first bear market, they separate absolutely: the neglectful panic, because they never knew what they owned. The still hold, because they never stopped knowing.

And stillness is not permanence. The map still rules, Chapter 23's structural reasons still trigger action, immediately and without sentiment, when the evidence demands it. The discipline is that evidence is the only trigger left. Not price or boredom.

> *Druckenmiller, the most aggressive great investor of his generation, the man who told us to go for the jugular, described his actual life as long stretches of doing absolutely nothing punctuated by rare, violent action when the fat pitch arrived.*

The jugular moments of Chapter 9 and the stillness of this chapter are one system: you can only strike hard because you were not busy, and you can only afford to be not busy because you know you will strike when it matters.

Tenet 24 says it plainly; one or two truly great decisions every few years is enough. The rest of the calendar is holding and waiting, with ongoing verification system in place. That is the job. It only looks like the absence of one.

The ring taught me that the wild swing is the one that gets you countered.

The fighter who throws at everything gasses out and walks onto the punch he never saw coming. The disciplined one keeps his guard, moves his feet, and waits for the opening that is actually there. Stillness in a portfolio is that posture exactly. You are guarded, refusing to swing at noise, waiting for the shot the market eventually hands to the patient.

Engineering Calm

Because willpower fails, the professionals build stillness structurally. The methods are unglamorous and they work.

Widen the reporting period, as Chapter 24 prescribed, quarterly inspection as the scheduled ritual, daily prices demoted to weather. Delete the frictionless pathways: price alerts off, trading app off the phone home screen; every step added between impulse and execution is compounding protected.

Keep the one-page thesis of Chapter 9 current for every position, so that when the itch arrives dressed as analysis, there is a document, written by the calm you, to argue with.

Pre-commit your triggers in writing: what evidence sells, what panic deploys the chest, everything else waits for the quarterly review. And give the restlessness somewhere harmless to live, the watch list absorbs infinite research energy without endangering a single compounding position. Study constantly. Transact rarely.

The sleep test at this altitude, one more time: down 10% on $10,000 is annoying; down 10% on $1.5 million is $150,000, a year of a good salary, gone in a red week. The knowledge from Part III is what lets you sleep. The structure from this chapter is what lets you not act, and at scale, those are the two halves of the entire remaining job.

Wealth is built in the buying and realized in the holding, and the holding is the decision, renewed in silence, every single day the world gives you a reason to break it.

Part IV, Chapter 26

Bear Markets: The Wealth Transfer

"Far more money has been lost by investors preparing for corrections, or trying to anticipate corrections, than has been lost in corrections themselves."

- Peter Lynch

Bear Markets: The Wealth Transfer

Every few years, the market conducts a census. It arrives disguised as a catastrophe, runs for months or years, and when it ends, the same shares exist, the same companies exist, but they have new owners.

> *This is the truth about bear markets that reframes everything: fear does not destroy wealth. It moves it. Every share sold in panic is bought, at that panic price, by someone who was prepared. The businesses go on; the factories, the software, the moats survive untouched; only the names on the ownership register change. A bear market is not a disaster that happens to the market. It is a transfer of assets from weak hands to strong ones, conducted at maximum speed, and the entire question of your investing life is which side of the transfer you have arranged to be on.*

Selling at the bottom is gifting your future gains to someone else, with the gift wrap of relief.

The Anatomy of the Wheel

Bears are not anomalies. They are the market's respiratory cycle, and every one follows a recognizable arc. I have now lived it twice at full scale, and the two could not have looked more different while being exactly the same.

- 2020 was the crash form: thirty percent gone in five weeks, the world closed, half of finance certain the economy was finished. Terrifying, and brief. The recovery began before most people finished panicking.

- 2022 was the grind form: no single day of horror, just twelve months of relentless decline. Inflation, rate hikes, war. My portfolio down 55% peak to trough, and every rally revealed as another trap. The grind is the crueler species, because it exhausts rather than shocks: month eight of red is where conviction goes to die, long after the adrenaline of month one has faded.

And then came the part of the cycle nobody discusses enough: the disbelief rally.

2023 opened with sentiment in the gutter and the crowd positioned for another leg down. And the market ground higher, month after month, while the scarred majority stayed out waiting for a re-entry signal that never came. By the time the public believed the recovery, the S&P had already run to new highs.

This is the standard exit from every bear: recovery arrives precisely when it is least believed, and the investors who sold in the despair phase get punished twice. Once by the selling, once by the disbelief that keeps them out through the restoration. Down 55% in 2022, my portfolio rose 131% in 2023 and 203% in 2024. Every share that produced those two years was owned before the turn, most of them bought during the despair itself.

Tenet 13 completes the wheel: every bull market sows the seeds of its own destruction. Booms breed excess optimism, overexpansion, overpaying, careless lending.

And the following bear is the controlled burn that clears it.

Which means the bear you are dreading is not a malfunction of the system. It is the system, doing maintenance, and redistributing ownership while it works.

The Playbook, Consolidated

Everything this book has built converges on the bear market, which is why the playbook is short. Every line is a chapter you have already read, arriving at its moment of use.

- **Before (which is always now):** the war chest filled and separate; the watch list researched in calm; the theses written; the balance sheets of every holding verified fortress-grade, because the companies that grip harder in recessions are chosen years in advance. Preparation is the entire edge, Chapter 21 forbade predicting the date, and the doctrine never needed it.

- **During:** run the Chapter 4 inspection: sway or structural failure, position by position, every month; the price will say catastrophe about everything, and the statements will tell you the truth about each. Hold everything the inspection clears. Deploy the chest in stages into the highest-conviction names as the despair deepens. Buying while bleeding, per the written plan, because the plan was written for exactly this weather. Expect it to feel wrong the entire time; March 2020 and late 2022 both felt, in the moment, like reinforcing a burning building. That feeling is the price tag on the returns.

- **Near the bottom:** which you will never identify in real time, and do not need to: the signals of maximum despair are behavioral, not technical. Capitulation headlines, the "investing is dead" essays, your own chest hitting zero against a market that keeps falling anyway. Mine emptied late 2022, close enough to the exact bottom that I claim no credit for timing, staged deployment into deepening fear lands you near bottoms automatically, without ever calling one.

- **After:** stay. The disbelief rally is the final exam, and its trick question is "shouldn't I wait for the retest?" The answer was Chapter 5: the recovery belongs to whoever is holding when it starts, and it always starts before permission is granted.

One reframe seals the chapter. You will endure perhaps eight or ten bear markets in an investing lifetime. Viewed one way, that is eight or ten ordeals. Viewed correctly, it is eight or ten scheduled wealth transfers, the only reliably recurring moments when decade-defining businesses are sold to you by their frightened owners at prices that assume the end of the world.

My money-weighted return runs at double my time-weighted return for exactly one reason: the heaviest capital of my life went in during the two transfers I have lived through. The bears did not interrupt the building of my portfolio.

The bears built it.

Panic is a market order placed by fear, filled by preparation. Decide, years in advance, which side of that fill you are.

Signs of Excessiveness and Extremism

A cheat sheet for reading the extremes. Treat these two lists as a thermometer: they do not give you the date, only the temperature. No single sign means much on its own, but when most of a column is lit at once, the crowd has reached an emotional extreme, and extremes are where the wealth transfer happens. Near a top, they are a reason to stop chasing and let the war chest build. Near a bottom, they are your permission to deploy it.

Signs of a market top (euphoria – caution)

1. A flood of new IPOs
2. Prices rising fast and without pause
3. Cheap, abundant credit and rising leverage
4. Euphoric, inescapable financial media
5. Very high trading volumes
6. Historically high P/E and EV/EBITDA multiples
7. Art and luxury markets booming
8. "This time is different" is declared out loud
9. Amateur investors piling into equities
10. Innovation tipping into euphoria
11. Social proof driving the herd

Signs of a market bottom (despair – opportunity)

1. No deals: mergers and venture capital freeze
2. The IPO window is shut
3. Low price-to-sales and EV/EBITDA multiples
4. Many companies trading below book value
5. Central banks easing for six to twelve months
6. Recession declared, the news is stale
7. Yesterday's favourite sectors now hated
8. Credit available only to the safest borrowers
9. Investors cautious and out of the market
10. Grim newspaper and magazine covers
11. Depressed consumer sentiment

Part IV, Chapter 27

Resisting the Shiny Object

"The main thing is to keep the main thing the main thing."

- Stephen Covey

Resisting the Shiny Object

Every level of wealth has its own recruiter.

> *At $50,000, it is the options guru showing screenshots of weekly doubles. At $300,000, the crypto cycle, arriving on schedule with a new vocabulary and the same promise. At seven figures, it gets a better wardrobe: private deals, exotic structures, the leveraged strategy your new golf partner swears by, angel allocations offered because you are now "sophisticated."*

The costume upgrades with your net worth. The pitch never changes: your careful system is leaving money on the table, and everyone else is collecting it.

This chapter is about the most underrated skill in wealth-building. Staying in your lane while the lane next to you appears to be moving faster.

Why the Shine Works on You

Understand the mechanism, because the shiny object preys on intelligent, successful investors with surgical precision, through three vectors.

Envy with survivorship bias. You will only ever hear from the winners. The person who 20x'd a meme position posts daily; the two hundred who evaporated are silent. Your information diet about every hot strategy is a curated highlight reel assembled by the survivors, a distortion so reliable you should treat any strategy you learned about through its winners as unevaluated.

Boredom. Chapter 25's stillness has a side effect: done correctly, this system is monotonous for years at a stretch.

Verify, hold, wait. Meanwhile the shiny thing offers daily dopamine, action, a scoreboard that updates hourly. Much of what masquerades as strategy-switching is simply entertainment-seeking. The tinkering instinct of Chapter 25, dressed for a night out.

The feeling of being late. The most powerful vector of all, and the one Tenet 21 answers with a scalpel: if it feels easy and obvious, you are probably too late.

Real opportunities feel wrong at the start: uncomfortable, uncertain, lonely. Palantir at seven dollars felt like catching a falling knife, and Hims in the forgotten-SPAC desert felt like exhuming one. The opportunity everyone can see, that requires no research and only courage to chase, is not an opportunity. It is an exit, yours, being sold to you as an entrance. By the time the shine reaches you, the people who created it are distributing.

The Casino Audit

Run each recruit through the Chapter 1 test, because every shiny object fails it identically: would you still want this if the market closed for five years?

Options are the cleanest demonstration. When you own a great company's stock, time is your employee. The business compounds while you sleep, and you can be early, wrong on timing, and still triumphant. An option is the same thesis with an expiration date stapled to it: now you must be right about the company and the quarter, and every passing day is a withdrawal from your account.

Time, your only structural edge, converted into your enemy, for a fee. The same audit dismantles the rest of the parade: leverage converts sway into structural failure by making Chapter 4's temporary declines permanently fatal; the trendy sector is a candle that burns fast and burns out; the exotic instrument you cannot explain to a teenager is, per the definition of risk as ignorance, the riskiest holding available to you at any price.

None of this requires the shiny things to be scams. Most are legitimate games, that other people, with other edges, sometimes win. The point is narrower and harder: they are not your game, and every dollar and hour they recruit is deducted from the game you have spent years building an actual edge in.

Consistency Kills

Here is the arithmetic the shiny object never shows you, and it is the whole case.

The compounding tables of Chapter 3 have a hidden assumption baked into every row: the same strategy, uninterrupted, for the entire period.

Twenty percent for fifteen years only produces its miracle if the fifteen years are consecutive. The strategy-hopper never gets the miracle because each switch resets the clock: eighteen months in the hot thing, a drawdown, a chastened return, re-entry at worse prices, conviction rebuilt from zero.

Hop every three or four years and you can spend a lifetime earning decent returns in fragments that never compound into anything, while the plodding neighbor who did one thing for twenty years finishes with multiples of your result.

Consistency kills the competition. It is the least glamorous edge in markets and the least contested, because so few can stand to hold it. My own record in this book's appendix is not the product of brilliance evenly applied; it is one strategy, held through two bear markets, three manias I declined to attend, and roughly a thousand invitations to be more exciting.

And there is a heavier way to say it, the way I feel it: in long-term investing, there is no do-over. The eight years I have now spent on this one strategy are the only version of those eight years that will ever exist.

I cannot roll them back and try a different allocation of my twenties. That is pressure. It is also the liberation: commitment of that kind works like a marriage. You choose, and the choosing eliminates the noise, the alternatives, the daily renegotiation, the exhausting freedom of keeping every option open.

The strategy-hoppers are not just resetting their compounding clocks; they are living in a permanent state of proposal, never married to anything long enough for the vows to pay. Commit. Eliminate the distractions by making them irrelevant. The years are being spent either way, the only question is whether they accumulate into one structure or scatter across many foundations, none finished.

The defense is not willpower. It is having already answered the question. You know your game: seven to twelve great businesses, bought with evidence, held for decades, financed by a chest that feeds on panic. A system you understand completely, with a written record of why it works and receipts that it does. The recruiter's pitch has no purchase on someone who is not shopping.

Every fortune is guarded by a thousand exciting alternatives to the thing that is working.

Let the parade pass. You are not missing out, you are compounding, which is the one thing the parade will never do.

Part IV, Chapter 28

The Investor Skill Tree

"Your knowledge must grow with your portfolio, or your portfolio will shrink to match your knowledge."

The Investor Skill Tree

Years before I invested, I fought. Kickboxing, and what the ring teaches you about skill is worth more to an investor than a finance degree.

> *Nobody trains "kickboxing." You train the jab, the hook, the takedown defense, the footwork, the endurance. Dozens of small, nameable sub-skills, each one drillable, each one testable. And one day you notice they have fused into the big skill that has no drill of its own. Every serious craft works this way. And "being a great long-term investor" is exactly such a big, slightly vague skill. Which means it decomposes into a finite list of learnable parts, and the vagueness that intimidates beginners dissolves into a curriculum.*

This chapter is that curriculum: the complete map of what this book has installed, organized as a skill tree you can audit yourself against. It exists for two reasons.

First, so you can locate yourself, mark what you know, what needs refinement, what remains.

Second, because of the law this book's Chapter 3 tables encoded and my whole record demonstrates: your knowledge must grow with your portfolio, or your portfolio will shrink to match your knowledge. The 10, 15, and 20 percent rows of the compounding table are not luck tiers. They are competence tiers.

Branch One: Portfolio Management

The most commonly skipped branch, and therefore the first one: people collect stocks for years without ever managing a portfolio. Its sub-skills: the optimal number of holdings and why both three and sixty are wrong (Ch. 7); position sizing, from starter through built, and scaling in and out with a written plan (Ch. 9); cash management by portfolio size, and the war chest doctrine (Ch. 8); sector and size concentration awareness; the scaling plan across stages, how a $20k, $200k, and $2M portfolio are managed differently (Ch. 3, 24); hedging, and why reasonable cash is the only hedge this system needs; tax awareness as friction favoring the long hold (Ch. 23); and the portfolio's place among your other assets.

Branch Two: The Qualitatives

The judgment branch: what makes a business worth owning before any number is consulted. Moat identification across the seven types and moat trajectory, deepening or eroding (Ch. 10). Management evaluation: founders and skin in the game, the incentives in the proxy, the three-year promise ledger, conference-call listening (Ch. 11). Business model quality: asset-light versus asset-heavy and what each implies (Ch. 16). Competitive structure, the five-forces habit of asking who has the power in an industry. Supertrend location and the trend/supertrend distinction (Ch. 12). Total addressable market, honestly estimated. And the funnel itself, watch list discipline, staged research, the 99 no's (Ch. 13).

Branch Three: The Financials

The literacy branch. The income statement as a story: the waterfall, the golden relationships, operating leverage, one-time item stripping, the quarterly grade (Ch. 14). The balance sheet: fortress versus fragile, debt maturities, what the equity is made of (Ch. 15). The cash flow statement: free cash flow as truth serum, the net-income-versus-cash check (Ch. 15). Share count mechanics: dilution, buybacks, the stock-comp treadmill. The financial engineering catalog, recognized on sight. And the 10-K, read efficiently, twenty pages of signal in two hours (Ch. 17).

Branch Four: Valuation

The pricing branch, and the one that separates tiers most sharply. Basic ratios and, more important, which ratio fits which company type, the Amazon lesson (Ch. 18). Advanced ratios: free cash flow yield, ROIC, PEG. The Lynch rule and the multiple-versus-growth matrix (Ch. 18). Revenue and net income modeling; margin estimation as the pivotal assumption (Ch. 19, 16). Full projections with bull, base, and bear cases, maintained quarterly (Ch. 19). Comparative valuation across peers. The special cases: cyclicals, IPOs in the desert, turnarounds and their base rates (Ch. 22). Capital allocation grading: the six doors and the allocator's record (Ch. 20).

Branch Five: The Economy

Smallest branch, lowest priority, by design (Ch. 21): market cycles as recurring weather; rates as gravity on multiples; the specific macro forces touching your specific companies, and the trained reflex of ignoring everything else. Mastery here is mostly subtraction.

The Training Plan

Now the schedule, because a map without a timeline is decoration.

The goal is front-loaded: within roughly your first three years, command 80 percent of this tree.

That sounds aggressive and is deliberate, an hour or two a day of statements read, calls heard, projections attempted, post-mortems written. The reason for the urgency is Chapter 3's rotation: in the early years, capital matters more than skill, which makes those years the cheapest tuition you will ever get. Mistakes at $30,000 are lessons; the same mistakes at $900,000 are catastrophes. My own 52% loss in year one cost a few thousand dollars and paid for itself hundreds of times over. Build the competence while incompetence is still affordable.

And then never stop, because the tree is a ratchet with a leak: every branch decays without use, and every new portfolio scale (Ch. 24) demands the tree be re-learned at altitude.

The audit ritual: once a year, walk the five branches and let the gaps set next year's study plan. Fighters watch tape of their own fights. Your tape is your decision journal and your post-mortems, and it never lies about which sub-skill lost you the round.

The market pays every investor precisely once per skill, and then forever, compounding, for the whole tree.

Train like it. The version of you at level six of wealth is built from the drills the current version chooses this year.

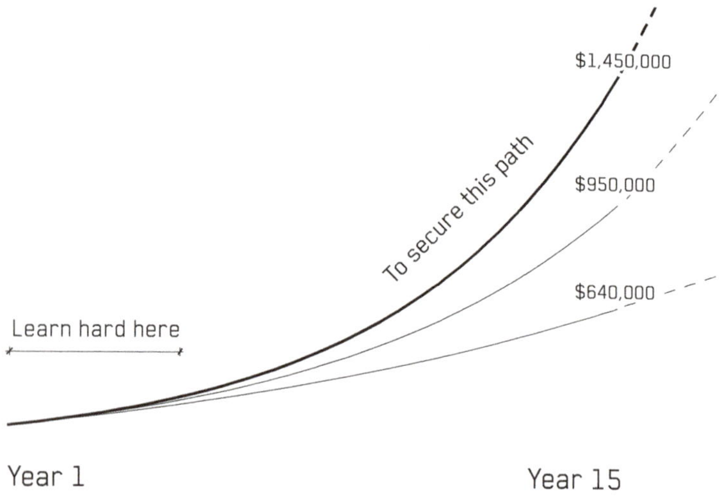

Part IV, Chapter 29

The Ten Levels of Wealth

"Seek wealth, not money or status. Wealth is having assets that earn while you sleep."

- Naval Ravikant

The Ten Levels of Wealth

A number on a brokerage screen is just a number. What can it do?

> *That is the question this chapter answers, because the destination of this whole book deserves a map with named places on it. Wealth is not a smooth continuum, it moves in levels, and each level changes something concrete: your exposure, your options, your relationship to work, your power over your own time.*

Place yourself on the map honestly, choose the level you are building toward, and give it a date. This is the practical form of Chapter 6's dated target.

Not "rich someday," but "level six within fourteen years," with the trifecta arithmetic that makes it real. We are building our future, not dream about abstract.

The figures below are liquid assets, calibrated to today; inflation will push every threshold upward over the decades, so treat the structure as permanent and the numbers as this era's edition.

The Climb: Levels 1–4

- Level 1 – $0 to $50k. Survival mode, stated without romance. Employment is mandatory, every dollar matters, and you are exposed to everything: employers, prices, institutions. Power: essentially none. The doctrine here is Chapter 3's first phase in its purest form: brute force. Maximize income, minimize leakage, feed the machine, and ascend as fast as possible while building the skill tree, because this is the level where mistakes are cheapest.

- Level 2 – $50k to $150k. Still dependent on employment, and now defense matters as much as offense: a single foolish move, or a medical bill, a wrecked car, can knock you back a level. Disciplined money management is the entire game. The compounding is real but not yet felt.

- Level 3 – $150k to $300k. The first interior shift: compounding becomes something you feel. A 20% year on $200k adds $40,000, the abstract chart from Chapter 3 starts happening to you personally, and the motivation problem of the early years solves itself. Optionality: still none. Power: still minimal. But the machine is now audibly running.

- Level 4 – $300k to $1M. Stability. Employment remains necessary, but financial stress fades and day-to-day life is solid. This is where much of the diligent middle class plateaus: the 401(k), the index funds, the okay-ish comfort. This level's great danger is precisely its comfort: it is a fine place to pass through and a costly place to park. Decisions can be made without immediate financial pressure. Power extends to the walls of your own household.

The Prize: Levels 5–7

- Level 5 – $1M to $2M. The threshold where money genuinely starts working for you, part-time work becomes conceivable, depending on your costs and cash flows. And note what the level certifies: reaching it within 10–20 years, rather than 40, means you know what you are doing. Time-plus-index gets some people here eventually; competence gets you here while it still matters. And let me set the bar: for someone working on building their wealth aggressively and actively (real savings rate, real skill development, real consistency) Level 5 within a decade is a demanding but entirely reasonable target. This is also the border of Chapter 24, the game changes here.

- Level 6 – $2M to $4M. The book's central promise: absent recklessness and foolishness, the foundation for lifelong prosperity is set. A portfolio this size can generate meaningful income from even conservative yields; catastrophe now requires actively inviting it.

- Level 7 – $4M to $10M. Full financial independence with margin. Work becomes entirely optional; geography, schedule, and attention become choices. Power extends to shaping your own time completely and small-scale economic outcomes around you, the level where the portfolio stops serving your life and starts underwriting other people's.

The Summit: Levels 8–10

- Level 8 – $10M to $25M. Wealth becomes structural: capital that directs the work of others: businesses funded, projects launched, meaningful decisions at scale. Getting here is rarely a byproduct of discipline alone; it requires elite competence in a specific domain and concentrated bets that worked.

- Level 9 – $25M to $70M. The same forces, an order of magnitude louder: ownership stakes that influence entire companies, capital that outlives its deployment cycles, and a name that opens rooms.

Almost always built on equity in something created, not only compounded.

- Level 10 – $70M+. Rare air: privacy and security at levels most people never see, and direct or indirect influence over markets, culture, capital. Noted for completeness (the map should show the whole territory) but this book was not written to get you here.

Reading the Map

Group the levels and the strategy clarifies. Levels 1-4 are the path: necessary, temporary, and not a destination; you may be there now, but do not plan to end there.

Levels 5-7 are the prize, and here is the sentence I most want this chapter to leave behind: levels 5 through 7 are achievable for essentially anyone who is reasonably disciplined and trains their judgment.

Not gifted or lucky. Not early to one miracle stock. Disciplined, for 10 to 20 years, with a competence that grows on the Chapter 28 schedule. These levels secure a comfortable life for you and your immediate family, and they should be your explicit, dated, minimum target.

Levels 8-10 are the summit. Possible but demanding a sharper plan than this book alone.

Then make it operational, today: I am at level __, investing ____$ monthly, compounding at roughly __%, which puts level __ approximately __ years out. And if that date is unacceptable, the trifecta names your three levers. Almost everyone starts at level 1; I did, ten years ago, with $165 and one share of Apple. The climb is not reserved. It is simply unclaimed.

The levels are a map of what money can do. But somewhere around level 5, most climbers discover the map has been measuring the wrong thing all along, and that discovery is the final chapter of this book.

Time, judgment, improvement. Nothing more is required, and nothing less has ever worked.

Part IV, Chapter 30

Building Something That Outlives You

"A society grows great when old men plant trees whose shade they shall never sit in."

- Greek proverb

Building Something That Outlives You

Every architect eventually confronts the same strange fact about the profession: the building will outlive its maker.

The blueprints are yours, the decisions are yours, the years of work are yours, and then the structure stands for a century, sheltering people who will never know your name.

Architecture is, at its core, the discipline of building for occupants you will never meet.

So is this.

We have reached the final chapter, and I owe you the truth about what you have been constructing. It was never just a portfolio.

The Artifact of Transformation

Return to the sentence planted in Chapter 24, because the whole book has been walking toward it: you will not remember the price you paid. You will remember the person you had to become to hold it.

Look at the record in Appendix B one last time, but read it differently now. The 52% loss in year one is the tuition receipt of a beginner who chose to stay. The 2022 line, minus 55% while buying every month, is not a drawdown, it is documentary evidence that a specific person had, by then, built the stomach, the knowledge, and the structure to act against every instinct evolution installed.

The 131% and 203% years are what the market paid that person, retroactively, for who he had become in the dark years before.

A seven-figure portfolio built through competence is not primarily a pile of money. It is an artifact, the physical proof that a transformation occurred. The discipline that survives level 2, the judgment trained across a hundred 10-Ks, the calm that holds through a grinding bear: those were the actual construction project. The portfolio is just where the evidence accumulated.

And here is why this distinction is the most practical paragraph in the book, not the most sentimental: the money can be lost, in principle, by anyone. The person cannot be. Hand the transformed investor a market crash, a fresh start, even a confiscation, and the same structure gets rebuilt, faster, because the builder still exists. Hand the untransformed heir a fortune, and the fortune finds its way back out. This is the mechanism behind the oldest proverb about wealth: shirtsleeves to shirtsleeves in three generations. What evaporates between the generations was never the money.

It was the builder.

What You Pass On

Which brings us to inheritance, and to the design problem almost every wealthy family gets wrong.

> *The default plan is to transfer the artifact: the accounts, the shares, the number. But you now know what the number is made of: decades of decisions, held by a person the decisions built. And you know that transferring the output without the transformation is transferring a building to someone who has never seen a load calculation. The market will conduct its census, as it always does, and the unprepared owner will be on the paying side of the transfer.*

So the estate plan of a competent investor has two layers, and the legal documents are the lesser one.

The greater one is teaching the system. The frameworks

of this book are all transferable: risk as ignorance, the war chest, the funnel, the stillness. They transfer the way every craft does: explained and practiced beside someone, years before the stakes are real.

Let your children watch you run a quarterly inspection. Let them hear you decline a mania out loud, and explain why the boredom is the strategy. Give a teenager a small real portfolio and the Chapter 28 tree, and let them pay cheap tuition at level zero, the same cheap tuition your first years paid. What compounds across generations is not capital.

It is judgment, installed early enough to protect the capital.

And notice, this is the quiet purpose of the book in your hands. Thirty chapters ago, this was a manual for building your portfolio. Read again in ten years, it is the curriculum for the person you will teach.

Write your own version: the decision journal, the post-mortems, the one-page theses. The most valuable document you can leave attached to a portfolio is the record of the thinking that built it.

The Building Rises

One last time, stand back and look at what the four parts of this book assembled.

The ground survey taught you which game to play and why the board tilts toward the patient. The foundation poured concentration, the war chest, and sizing into load-bearing doctrine. The structure gave you the engineering (statements, moats, valuations) that turns conviction from a mood into a calculation. And the building rises: through the changed game, the stillness, the bears that transfer rather than destroy, the levels that name what it is all for.

None of it required genius. Every chapter, you may have

noticed, required the same three materials in different mixtures: time, judgment, and the discipline to keep showing up. That is the entire recipe, and it has never once been improved upon, only abandoned, by people who wanted the building without the years.

> *You now hold the complete blueprint. The market opens tomorrow. Indifferent, generous, and rigged ever so slightly in favor of exactly the kind of owner these pages were written to build.*

Build something that lasts. Build something that outlives you.

Then teach someone to hold it, because that, and not the number, is the inheritance.

EPILOGUE

Cabo, 2040

It is a Tuesday afternoon in 2040, and you are on a terrace above the water.

The light has gone long and gold, the way it does in the last hour before dinner. Somewhere behind you, people you love are arguing pleasantly about where to eat. Your phone is inside, in a drawer, because Tuesday is not a day that requires you anymore. None of them are, particularly. That was the point, although you had almost forgotten there ever was a point, the way you forget the address of a building once you live in it.

You think about the market for a moment, the way you might think about weather in a country you used to live in.

There was a crash a few years back, a real one, the kind the anchors called historic. You remember it mostly because of how little you remember it. The inspection ran, the structure held, the chest emptied into the fear the way it had twice before, and the whole thing joined the long line of emergencies that turned out to be Tuesdays. Somewhere in the world right now, someone is panic-selling a great company to a stranger with a written plan. You know both people. You have been both people, but not for a long time.

The number, if you checked, would be large. You do not check it. This is the strangest part, the one the person who started with $165 and one share could never have believed: past a certain point, the number stopped being the thing. It never had been. It was only ever evidence of the person you had to become to earn it.

The judgment, trained across a hundred quiet evenings with filings no one made you read. The stomach, forged in a year that cut everything in half and could not make you flinch. The stillness, which everyone mistook for doing nothing and which was, you now understand, the hardest work you ever did.

You built a portfolio, and the portfolio built you back. That was the trade, the real one, hiding underneath eight thousand days of prices.

Down the years behind this terrace stand all the versions of you that had to hold: the beginner in the minus-52-percent winter, deciding to stay. The one buying through the grind while friends asked careful questions. The one who said no to a thousand shiny parades, who reread a thesis at 3 a.m. and closed the laptop and slept. None of them are here tonight. All of them are; load-bearing, every one, in a structure that no longer shows its scaffolding.

Someone calls your name from inside. Dinner has been decided, apparently, without you, the small democracies of a full life. You stand, and take one more look at the water.

Wall Street rented the decades by the quarter. You owned them.

The compounding was never the money. It was you.

Now go, you were told, a long time ago, on the first page of an old book, to build something that lasts.

You did.

Appendix A - 25 Tenets

The 25 Tenets

One canonical set. Each tenet is a compressed chapter; the references point to where the full argument lives.

1. Your edge does not come from Wall Street's experts. It comes from your own knowledge of specific companies, industries, and the world in its entirety. You can beat the experts by being grounded and in tune with society and its changes. (Ch. 1, 5)

2. The market's domination by professionals, algorithms, and index funds makes it easier for you, not harder. The giants are constrained, by quarters, by benchmarks, by career risk. By making your own decisions on your own clock, you play a game they are not allowed to enter. (Ch. 2, 5)

3. Owning stock makes you part owner of the company. Figure out what is going on in your company. Behave like an owner, because you are one. In a real sense, you sit above the CEO. (Ch. 2, 20)

4. Volatility is not risk. Risk is losing your money permanently. Your portfolio swinging 20% in a year is not risk if you own strong businesses. Sway is not structural failure. (Ch. 4)

5. Risk comes from not knowing what you are doing. The market does not forgive ignorance. Your job is to convert unknowns into knowns through competence. (Ch. 4)

6. Markets, rates, recessions, nobody gets it right every time. It is not possible to accurately

predict interest rates, the economy, or the market, so ignore the forecasts. What you can do is be positioned to survive whatever comes next. (Ch. 21)

7. A great business compounds its advantages over time. A mediocre one slowly rots. Good businesses build deeper moats, stronger brands, bigger customer bases every year. Own the right side of that divide. (Ch. 10)

8. The simplest businesses with the clearest runway usually win. You get no bonus points for owning something complicated. If you cannot explain the investment simply, you do not have an investment, you have a hope. Someone's tweet with rocket emojis does not count as research. (Ch. 13)

9. Concentrate your bets when you have an edge. There is no trophy for owning fifty stocks you barely understand. Under 7 companies is more than enough before six figures; 12 can safely carry you to a million and beyond. You are not trying to be kind of right on dozens of things, you are aiming to be dead right on a few. (Ch. 7)

10. You do not have to be invested at all times. If no company fits your criteria, park the money and wait. Cash with a plan is a position. (Ch. 8)

11. High returns are born in periods of low expectations. When the future looks bleak, valuations collapse, and that is where the biggest gains hide. The market rewards bravery, not comfort. (Ch. 8, 26)

12. Bear markets are when wealth transfers from weak hands to strong ones. Fear does not destroy

wealth, it moves it. Selling at the bottom is not just giving up your shares; it is gifting your future gains to someone else. (Ch. 26)

13. Every bull market sows the seeds of its own destruction. Nothing grows forever. Booms create excess optimism, overexpansion, overpaying, careless lending. Expect the winter; it is part of the climate. Market dips are as normal as snow in the Alps, prepare for them and they cannot harm you. (Ch. 2, 26)

14. The short-term price and the business are two different things. A company's stock may not match its operational success for years, and in the long run, the two are directly linked. That temporary disparity is what makes a successful investment. You do not make money by being right, but when others realize you were right. (Ch. 4, 22)

15. Accounting is the language of business. Many portfolios were ruined by companies with weak balance sheets and poor cash flow quality. Learn to read before you buy. (Ch. 14, 15)

16. Great businesses generate free cash flow. Mediocre ones generate promises. Revenue is easy; hype is easy. Actual surplus cash, year after year, cycle after cycle, is hard. If you cannot see the cash building up, it probably is not real. Real businesses send cash back to owners; dividends and smart buybacks prove the profits exist. (Ch. 15, 20)

17. Financial engineering can mask weak fundamentals, at least for a while. Buyback games, aggressive accounting, debt-fueled dividends create the illusion of health. But fundamentals do

not lie forever. Eventually, the bill comes due. (Ch. 15)

18. Watch how management gets paid. The mission statement sounds good; incentives tell the truth. Executives rewarded for a quarterly stock pop play short-term games. Executives rewarded for years of free cash flow growth create real value. (Ch. 11, 20)

19. A stretched valuation turns a good business into a bad investment. The company might be amazing. The management might be world-class. But if you pay too much, you still lose. Price always matters. (Ch. 18)

20. It is better to be roughly right than precisely wrong. You do not need perfect models or fifteen decimal points. Business is messy; investing is messy. Build ranges, not prophecies. (Ch. 19)

21. Be cautious with trendy stocks in trendy industries. The candle that burns fast burns out. If it feels easy and obvious, you are probably too late. Real opportunities feel wrong at the start. And the smaller the company, the more proof of performance you should demand. (Ch. 22, 27)

22. Most turnarounds do not turn. Broken businesses are usually broken for a reason, and in most cases decline is terminal. If you must fish in troubled industries, choose proven survivors and wait for actual signs of revival, the graveyard is full of inventions made obsolete. (Ch. 22)

23. Sell for solid reasons or not at all. A decline in the company's financial health is a reason. Temporary market fluctuations, negative headlines,

and round-number gains are not. There will always be concerns; that is not information. (Ch. 23)

24. Time is your employee in stocks and your enemy in options. Owning quality companies gives you the luxury of patience. You can be early, wrong on timing, and still triumphant. Options carry an expiration date; long shots rarely pay, and all returns must be risk-adjusted. One or two truly great decisions every few years is enough. Systems beat predictions. (Ch. 5, 25, 27)

25. Outperformance is a decision, and thorough work is how it is paid for. If you will not pay, index honestly, expect market returns, and sleep well. A valid choice, made by an honest person. If you aim for 20 percent and beyond, the due diligence is required. Investing is exhilarating, mentally stimulating, and dangerous without it.(Ch. 1, 6)

Twenty-five sentences, one system. If the book ever leaves your shelf, these pages are the part to keep in your pocket.

Appendix B - The Record
2018-2026

Every number in this book comes from the ledger below.

- One portfolio
- One strategy
- One hundred and two months
- No withdrawals, nothing omitted.

It begins with the worst year I ever had, because a record that starts after the mistakes is not a record. It is marketing.

FIRST ENTRY - JANUARY 2018	$165 / €145
PORTFOLIO - JUNE 2026	€2,378,353
WAR CHEST	- €350,000
DEPOSITED SINCE 2018	€442,940
TIME-WEIGHTED RETURN	24.2% / yr
MONEY WEIGHTED RETURN (XIRR)	51.5% / yr
ONE DOLLAR, START TO FINISH	$6.20

Source: monthly brokerage records since inception.

Time-weighted return computed as chain-linked monthly Modified Dietz returns, deposits weighted mid-month (beginning-of-month treatment yields 36%); money-weighted return as XIRR on dated deposits.

Original portfolio statements and calculations made in EUR.

The Year-by-Year Ledger

YEAR	DEPOSITED	YEAR END VALUE	RETURN
2018	€12,665	€10,809	-52.0%
2019	€11,122	€34,410	+67.2%
2020	€51,361	€147,093	+9.4%
2021	€31,490	€251,375	+46.2%
2022	€44,166	€137,465	-55.3%
2023	€98,290	€443,011	+131.1%
2024	€32,782	€1,400,567	+202.9%
2025	€116,000	€2,621,331	+73.4%
2026 (YTD)	€45,200	€2,378,353	-11.0%

Read the deposit column against the return column and the doctrine of Chapter 8 becomes visible: the heaviest capital of every stretch went in during or immediately after the red years. The losses are printed in red at full size.

Annual figures are time-weighted (Modified Dietz, chain-linked monthly), independent of deposit timing. 2026 is year-to-date through end of June.

The Doctrine, Measured

Two return figures describe the same portfolio. The distance between is the war chest doctrine of Chapter 8, expressed as arithmetic.

TIME-WEIGHTED RETURN	24.2% / yr
MONEY WEIGHTED RETURN	51.5% / yr

The gap exists because capital did not arrive evenly. It arrived when the market was bleeding. The chest emptied to zero exactly twice, into the crash of 2020 and the bear of 2022. The money-weighted figure is the market's receipt for that timing.

EVERY DEPOSIT INTO S&P 500	≈ €720,000
PORTFOLIO - JUNE 2026	€2,378,353
THE DIFFERENCE	≈ €1.65M

What if I just bought the index?

Identical money, identical dates, identical discipline. The only variable was what the money bought. This is what the work was worth.

About the author

Ondrej Slunecko is a long-term investor. He practices what this book teaches: a concentrated portfolio of deeply researched businesses, held for years, documented in full.

He began in January 2018 with $165, studying architecture in Denmark and washing dishes to fund the deposits. The early conviction positions (Tesla, Palantir, Hims & Hers, SoFi) and the record they produced are printed, year by year, losses included, in Appendix B. By his late twenties, the portfolio had crossed seven figures, several times over.

Today he is a Managing Director of Jeremy Lefebvre's Private Stock & Wealth Group and 1000xStocks research platform, where he helps investors improve decision-making, capital allocation, and long-term portfolio compounding.

He still reads every 10-K himself.

An Invitation

This book is the complete system and a disciplined reader can take these pages and implement.

But there is a difference between owning the blueprints and building alongside other builders. The years documented in this book did not happen alone. They happened inside a community of serious investors, arguing about the same filings, holding through the same winters, checking each other's work. That community exists, and it is open.

The Private Stock & Wealth Group, more than 3,000 investors, is where the system in this book operates live: the research process of Part III applied to real companies every week, earnings seasons worked through as they happen, projections built and maintained in the open, and questions answered by people who hold real positions, myself included.

It is also where the education continues past the last page – over one hundred hours of video masterclasses covering everything this book taught, at full depth.

If that is the kind of room you want to be in, or if you simply want to reach me, everything is at:

ondrejslunecko.com

www.ingramcontent.com/pod-product-compliance
Lightning Source LLC
LaVergne TN
LVHW071049081126
851858LV00027B/133
9780809987067